A
D.H. Lawrence
Album

A
D. H. LAWRENCE
ALBUM

by

George Hardy
and
Nathaniel Harris

MOORLAND PUBLISHING

British Library Cataloguing in
Publication Data

A D.H. Lawrence album.
1. Lawrence, D.H. — Biography 2.
Authors, English — 20th century
— Biography
I. Hardy, George II. Harris,
Nathaniel
823'.912 PR6023.A93Z/

ISBN 0 86190 063 4

To
Violet Hardy
and
Rosie Harris

Printed in the UK by
Billings and Sons Ltd,
Worcester.
Published by
Moorland Publishing Co Ltd,
Station Street,
Ashbourne, Derbyshire,
DE6 1DE England.
Tel: (0335) 44486

Contents

Introduction

Even more than most writers, D.H. Lawrence used his own life as the raw material of his fiction. His novels and stories are crowded with descriptions of places he knew, characters he had met, and incidents that had actually occurred. Almost all his significant work is grounded in such transcribed realities, however much he subsequently developed characters and situations along distinctively 'Lawrentian' lines.

Lawrence's material was abundant, since he lived intensely and travelled restlessly from place to place (in a sense, he never had a home after the death of his mother). His wanderings gave him the settings for stories and travel books, and also for novels such as *Kangaroo* (Australia, Cornwall) and *The Plumed Serpent* (Mexico). Most of his friends and acquaintances eventually turned up in his writings as recognizable, life-like portraits or equally recognizable caricatures. And Lawrence's marriage-struggle with his 'Queen Bee', Frieda, is played over again and again in his writings, where the dissatisfied older woman eternally loves and fights against the small, dark, passionate man, who represents Lawrence or Lawrence-as-he-might-have-been.

But the materials Lawrence used most exhaustively — and most directly of all — were taken from an earlier setting: from Eastwood, the Nottinghamshire mining town where he was born, and from the countryside he loved so much — 'the country of my heart' to the north of the town. These comprise 'the Lawrence country', and as the photographs in this book demonstrate, he wrote of it, and of its people, with loving attention to detail. His descriptions of persons and events were often so faithful to reality, and so easy to identify, that he was lucky not to face actions for libel. (Such an action was in fact threatened by the husband of his friend Alice Hall, whom Lawrence put into *The White Peacock*, absurdly under-disguised as 'Alice Gall'.) This literalness is most pronounced in the novels *Sons and Lovers, The Lost Girl, The White Peacock, Aaron's Rod* and *Women in Love*, and in a cluster of 'Lawrence country' short stories. Here are a few examples:

Sons and Lovers, as is well known, holds close to the realities of the Lawrence family's history and Lawrence's own upbringing in 'Bestwood' — so close that some biographers have not hesitated to go to the book for their facts. It is hard to blame them. The drunken miner, Morel, and his resentful 'ladylike' wife are certainly Lawrence's own parents;

the passionate mother-and-son relationships actually existed; Paul Morel is Lawrence himself in all but a few externals; and the life and death of Paul's gifted older brother, William, follows that of the Lawrences' second son, Ernest. The agony of Paul Morel, unable to find salvation in either a spiritual relationship with Miriam Leivers or sexual passion with Clara Dawes, resembles Lawrence's situation vis-à-vis Jessie Chambers and Alice Dax; and, like Morel, he had still to face a struggle for self-liberation after the death of his mother.

In the early part of *The Lost Girl*, Lawrence makes equally free with the history of another Eastwood family. These chapters describe the lives of a draper, James Houghton, and his daughter Alvina; this time the town is 'Woodhouse'. Almost every verifiable detail corresponds to the known history of the Eastwood draper George Henry Cullen and his daughter Flossie. Cullen and his wife, Flossie and her governess, and even Cullen's live-in shop manageress appear in the novel as they did in life. (Lawrence did, however, eliminate Flossie's brother — not, as has sometimes been stated, a sister — in order to concentrate attention on his heroine.) The series of ill-starred business ventures undertaken by Houghton also occurred — to Cullen — exactly as Lawrence described them: first the failing shop, then the little windlass pit, finally the out-of-town cinema. The pit, Throttle-ha'penny, went into *The Lost Girl* without even a change of name.

Throttle-ha'penny and Alice Hall/Gall are two among many possible examples of Lawrence's odd reluctance to disguise his sources — as if, like primitive man, he felt there was a magic virtue even in the proper naming of names. Something of this is visible even in his first novel, *The White Peacock*, where the chief character, George Saxton, is clearly modelled on Jessie Chambers's brother Alan. Although George is not shown as living on the Chambers family's farm, the Haggs, Lawrence merely tilted the camera, so to speak, putting George down just a few fields away, at Felley Mill Farm; in the novel he calls it Strelley Mill — an echoing name that must itself have been taken from Strelley, which is further south and close to Cossall, where Lawrence's friend Louie Burrows lived.

Aaron's Rod opens in a patently real Eastwood townscape: we can trace Aaron's progress from his home in Lynn Croft (where his original lived next door to the Lawrences) to the public house across the road from Cocker House Lane, and on down the lane to Cocker House itself, a few hundred yards beyond Plumtre Colliery. The characters in this part of the novel — notably the pub's landlady and an Indian doctor, one of her customers — were well known in Eastwood.

There is more invention in *Women in Love*, but Lawrence nonetheless makes very free use of local people, places and events. One of the two male principals, Gerald Crich, is based on the mine-owner Philip Barber. With considerable audacity Lawrence included many authentic details about the Barbers, among them two family tragedies, an accidental shooting and a drowning, that had occurred only twenty years before.

Understandably, the Barbers were outraged — like many Eastwood folk of less public eminence, who also found versions of themselves and their doings in Lawrence's novels and stories. This — rather than the notoriety of *Lady Chatterley's Lover* — accounts for the long-felt hostility towards Lawrence's memory in his home town. Most of it has disappeared with the passage of generations, but even quite recently a group of colliers in a public house were overheard berating Lawrence. Their attitude was more sophisticated than that of their forebears: what made the man objectionable, they agreed, was not that he wrote up local tittle-tattle, but that he failed to check its accuracy before going into print! Which is a view one can have some sympathy with, even if it is not quite to the point as literary criticism.

Given the exceptionally close relationship between reality and fiction in Lawrence's work, photographs of the people and places he knew in his youth are bound to have a special fascination. The majority of the pictures in this book have never been published before; they are the fruit of many years' work on the part of George Hardy, who is well known as an Eastwood local historian. Some were passed across the counter to him at Eastwood Post Office, where George's job put him in an ideal position to contact pensioners who had interesting old 'snaps' tucked away; other finds were the results of careful research, persistence and serendipity.

As assembled by George Hardy, these images show that Lawrence's settings and descriptions tended to be even more meticulously literal and accurate than has been recognized until now. To name a few details at random, we find that Alvina Houghton's youngish governess did have grey-white hair; that Mr Braithwaite's original in *Sons and Lovers* did muffle himself in an enormous silk neckerchief; that 'William Morel' (Ernest Lawrence), hitherto seen only in stuffed-shirt photos, did look as jolly and vital as D.H. Lawrence claimed; and that William's 'Gipsy' fiancée was indeed a darkly handsome creature. One of the most striking of George Hardy's discoveries is the picture of Lucy Cullen in her 'black dress with a white lace collar fastened by a twisted gold brooch'. This is Lawrence's description of Mrs Houghton, the fictional counterpart of Lucy Cullen in *The Lost Girl*. It was written in 1913 and corresponds neatly to the photograph reproduced on page

72; what makes it of particular interest is that the woman herself died in 1904. This example of Lawrence's powerful visual memory makes it easier to believe Keith Sagar's assertion (in his *Life of D.H. Lawrence*) that Lawrence, having spent only a few days in Sardinia, left the island without making a single note for the travel book he subsequently published — *Sea and Sardinia*.

None of this should make us forget that Lawrence did write fiction, and was ready enough to diverge from 'reality' when his art or vision demanded it. One instance is worth noting, since it concerns a particularly impressive group of photographs. In *The Lost Girl*, Alvina Houghton trained as nurse, came home, and found herself playing the piano in her father's cinema. After his death she joined a theatrical troupe, took up with a darkly passionate Italian, submitted to him in the best Lawrentian wish-fulfilling style, and ended her fictional existence as a 'lost girl' in the alien mountains of southern Italy. The 'real' Alvina, Flossie Cullen, chose a less sensational course: she married the cinema's cashier, George Hodgkinson, and settled down at Percy Street in Eastwood.

The photographs in this book (with the exception of some well-known items included for the sake of comprehensiveness) come from the collection of George Hardy, who also did much of the research for the caption material. The words are mine. The text comprises a plain account of Lawrence's home and local background; it complements and threads together the pictorial evidence. The captions put names to the photographic images, and relate them to Lawrence's writings —those fictions which, paradoxically, give this exercise in historical reconstruction its most important reason for existing.

Nathaniel Harris

Fact into Fiction: 'AARON'S ROD'

Aaron's Rod, published in 1922, is full of lively, malicious portraits and caricatures of people Lawrence had met in Eastwood, London and Italy. In external details at least, the main character, Aaron Sisson, was suggested by Thomas Cooper, who lived on Lynn Croft in Eastwood. At the beginning of the book Sisson walks from his home to a pub, and later goes on to a fine house where he becomes involved with the occupants. As this group of photographs demonstrates, the places and people existed and were taken over into Lawrence's fictional world virtually unchanged.

1 The Avenue, Eastwood, more commonly known as Cocker House Lane; Cocker House stood at one end, and the Thorn Tree Inn at the other. Chapters II and III of *Aaron's Rod* exactly reproduce the topography of the area, though the names are changed. 'At one end of the dark, tree-covered Shottle Lane stood the Royal Oak public house....At the other end....was Shottle House....Shottle House stood two hundred yards beyond New Brunswick Colliery'.

2

3

4

2 Cocker House, which provided Lawrence with a model for Shottle House in *Aaron's Rod*. It was a 'pleasant, square house, rather old, with shrubberies and lawns'; notice the croquet lawn in front of the house.

3 The Thorn Tree Inn, at the top of Cocker Lane. In *Aaron's Rod,* Sisson enters Shottle Lane, where 'a lamp glimmered in front of the "Royal Oak". This was a low, white house sunk three steps below the highway.' Like the 'Royal Oak', the real pub was run by a woman, as the sign indicates.

4 Plumtre Colliery, the New Brunswick Colliery of the novel, photographed on the day it closed down in 1912.

5 **6**

5 Dr Russell, an Indian at Eastwood. Lawrence certainly had him in mind when writing in *Aaron's Rod* of Sherardy, 'the little doctor, who had lived for some years among the colliers, and become quite familiar with them'. He takes part in a discussion in the parlour of the 'Royal Oak', arguing that while Indians might well govern themselves worse than the British governed them, 'People should always be responsible for themselves.' Lawrence's portrait of Sherardy is not entirely sympathetic, although Dr Russell is said to have been well-respected in the locality.

6 Alfred Wolstan Brentnall and his family. The tyrant of the colliery offices in *Sons and Lovers* (where he appears as Mr Braithwaite, 'usually muffled in an enormous silk handkerchief'), Brentnall also figures in *Aaron's Rod*. The family lived at Cocker House; the aged 'Alfred Bricknell' was the patriarch of its fictional counterpart, Shottle House. The presence of a croquet hoop suggests that the photograph was taken on the lawn of Cocker House (see photograph 2). Brentnall was still alive when Lawrence published *Aaron's Rod*; he died in 1925, at the age of ninety-one.

I
Family Portrait

David Herbert Richards Lawrence — D.H. Lawrence — was born on 11 September 1885 at Eastwood, a little town of blackened red brick just over eight miles north-west of Nottingham. His father, Arthur John Lawrence, worked as a miner at his native Brinsley, one of the collieries scattered over the countryside around Eastwood. His mother, Lydia Lawrence, née Beardsall, was the daughter of an engineer — an admittedly elastic term in Victorian usage — and was ladylike and accomplished enough to have done a little teaching before her marriage.

D.H. Lawrence's parents were ill-matched, as *Sons and Lovers* records in painful detail. This was not a matter of class difference in the crude sense (their families were related by marriage before they met), but of upbringing and temperament. Arthur Lawrence was a simple

7 'Bert': D.H. Lawrence as a baby, 'a puny, fragile little specimen' according to William Hopkin, who met Mrs Lawrence pushing him in his pram; he looked 'like a skinned rabbit'.

man, feckless and barely literate, whose world was restricted to the pit, the pub and the home — probably in descending order of importance. His wife was a product of the Nonconformist tradition, with real aspirations to culture and refinement, a rigorous standard of

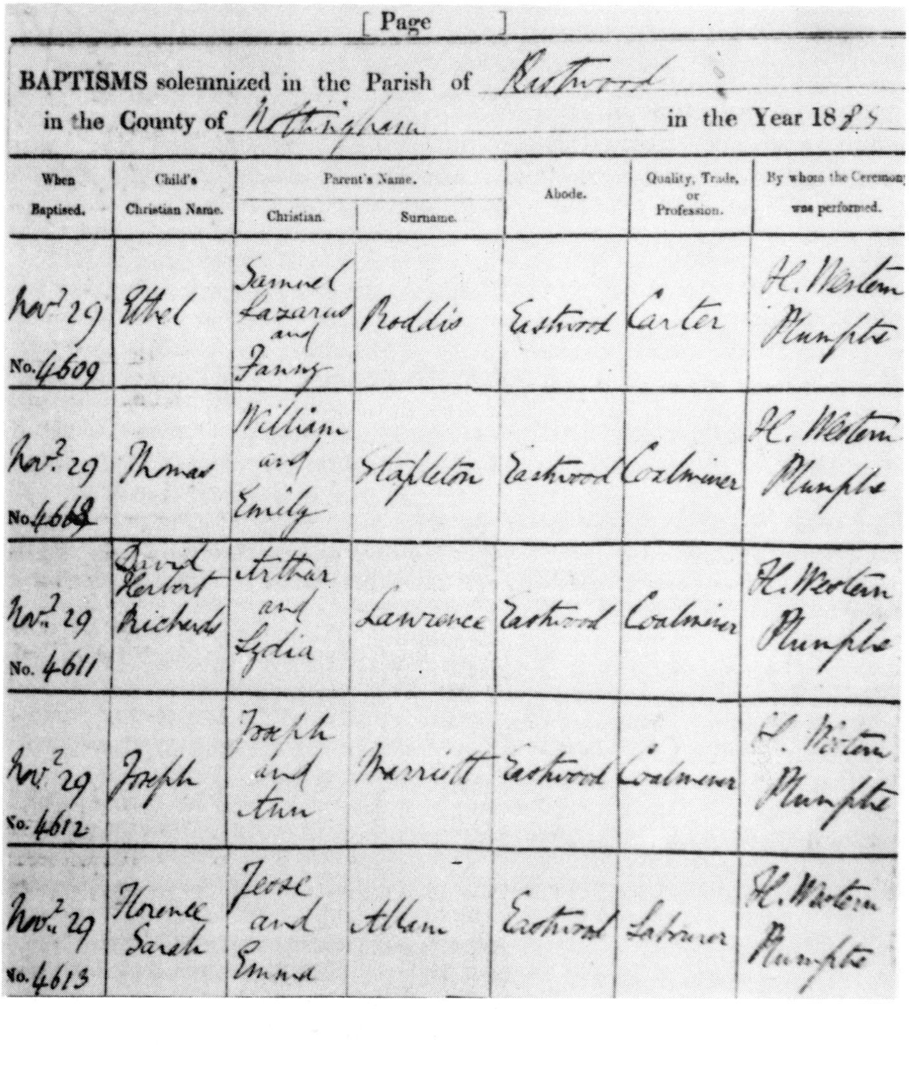
[Page]

BAPTISMS solemnized in the Parish of Eastwood in the County of Nottingham in the Year 1885

When Baptised.	Child's Christian Name.	Parent's Name. Christian	Parent's Name. Surname.	Abode.	Quality, Trade, or Profession.	By whom the Ceremony was performed.
Novr 29 No. 4609	Ethel	Samuel Lazarus and Fanny	Roddis	Eastwood	Carter	H. Weston Plumptre
Novr 29 No. 4610	Thomas	William and Emily	Stapleton	Eastwood	Coalminer	H. Weston Plumptre
Novr 29 No. 4611	David Herbert Richards	Arthur and Lydia	Lawrence	Eastwood	Coalminer	H. Weston Plumptre
Novr 29 No. 4612	Joseph	Joseph and Ann	Marriott	Eastwood	Coalminer	H. Weston Plumptre
Novr 29 No. 4613	Florence Sarah	Jesse and Emma	Allen	Eastwood	Labourer	H. Weston Plumptre

8 The record of D.H. Lawrence's baptism at St Mary's Church, Eastwood. On his marriage certificate his father described himself as a mining contractor; here he appears realistically as 'Coalminer', like most of the other fathers. The girl whose baptism is recorded at the top of the page, Ethel Roddis, is the mother of George Hardy, co-author of this book.

9

9 The Lawrence family: a studio portrait taken in Nottingham about 1894-5. Arthur and Lydia Lawrence sit with their children (left to right) Ada, Emily, George, Bert (D.H. Lawrence) and Ernest. The younger children look pretty gormless, perhaps because of the long exposure time needed for taking photographs in those days. This is very much a 'Sunday best' version of the family, free from pit-dirt and conflict — both of which figured largely in the Lawrences' lives. Interestingly, the miner is hale and hearty; his wife, six years younger, is worn down with work and might almost pass as his mother.

10 The Thurlby family. According to a local story, the Lawrences and their neighbours, the Thurlbys, went into Nottingham together to have themselves photographed. The men went ahead on foot, using the occasion as an excuse for a pub-crawl; the women and children followed in a cart. Of the two studio portraits taken that day at Phillips & Freckleton, only that of the Lawrences was known until George Hardy discovered this photograph.

financial responsibility, and a fierce distaste for dirt and drink. When the bloom wore off their relationship, the Lawrences found themselves hopelessly at odds. Arthur, who had 'taken the pledge' under Lydia's influence and sported the blue ribbon of the sworn teetotaller, looked for consolation in the jollity and cameraderie of the public house. Lydia turned to the children, who all took her side; her sons became surrogate husbands — whence the title of *Sons and Lovers*, which is very much Lydia's version of the family's history; only later in life did D.H. Lawrence realize that his father too had virtues and grievances.

Lawrence was the fourth child of Arthur and Lydia. The eldest, George, was born in 1876, followed by Ernest in 1878 and Emily in 1882. Lawrence — 'Bert' — arrived in 1885, and Ada in 1887. After that, though Mrs Lawrence was still only in her mid-thirties, there were no more children. Even as a baby Bert suffered from poor health: in the first winter of his life Lydia Lawrence confided to William Hopkin, whom she met on the street, that she did not expect the sickly little mite in the pram to live: 'I s'll never rear him.' But despite his frailty, Lawrence's hold on life — then and later — proved surprisingly strong.

II
The Eastwood Background

Early in their marriage the Lawrences lived in several little towns in the Nottingham mining country, and for a while they stayed at Brinsley. But by the time of Bert Lawrence's birth they had settled at Eastwood, which was to be their home for over thirty years.

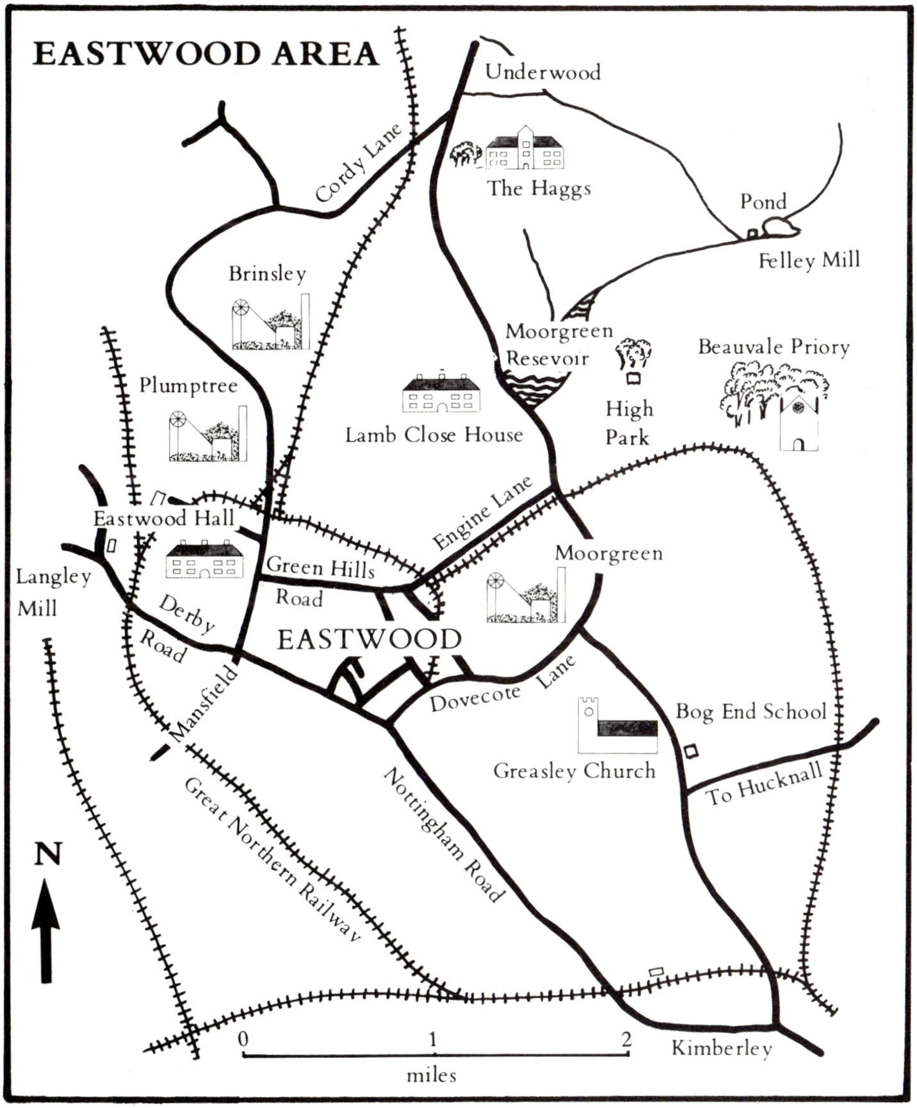

11 Edward Lionel Munro changed his surname to Walker-Munro on marrying Mabel Zoe Walker, heiress of the Walker mining family, in about 1890. The couple spent little time at Eastwood Hall. According to an inscription on the back of this curious and interesting photograph, Walker-Munro is its subject (in fancy dress?); and this is plausible since it was found along with a photograph of Dr Duncan McDonald Forbes (photographs 63-4), who administered the estate after Walker-Munro's death.

Eastwood is just inside Nottinghamshire, set among hills from which it looks down on the narrow little Erewash Valley; the Erewash, hardly more than a stream, is the boundary between Nottinghamshire and Derbyshire. The town consisted of shops and buildings strung out along the hilltop on the Nottingham Road, going in a roughly east-west direction. Below the road, on a slope running down towards the north, were the blocks of dull red-brick miners' houses. At the western end of the town was the market place, where the roads to Nottingham, Mansfield, Derby and Ilkeston all met; Brinsley, where Arthur Lawrence carried on working after the move to Eastwood, was on the Mansfield Road, just to the north.

12 The colliery at Brinsley. D.H. Lawrence's father was born in the village and worked down the pit there for most of his life.

13 Eastwood Hall, home of the Walker family, partners in the mine-owning firm of Barber, Walker & Co. It is now the National Coal Board Area Ofice.

EASTWOOD

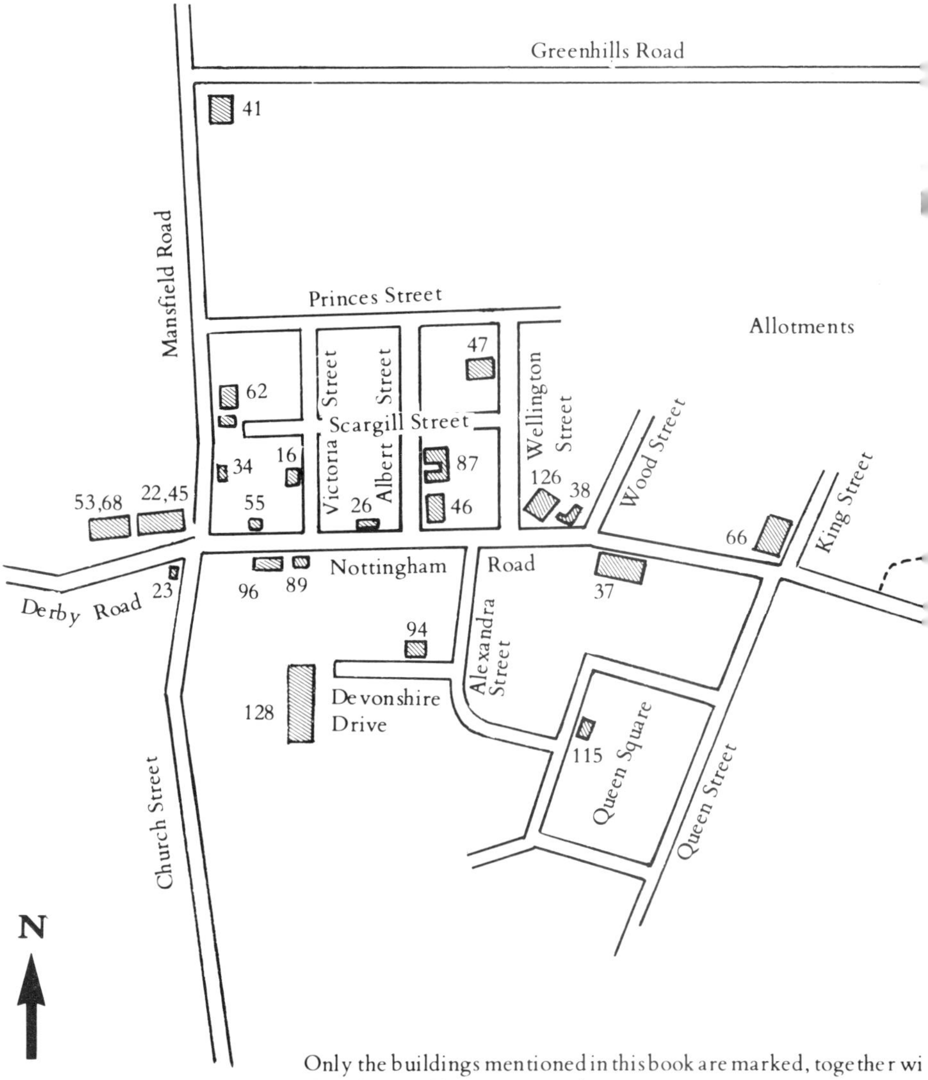

Only the buildings mentioned in this book are marked, together wi
the relevant illustration number.

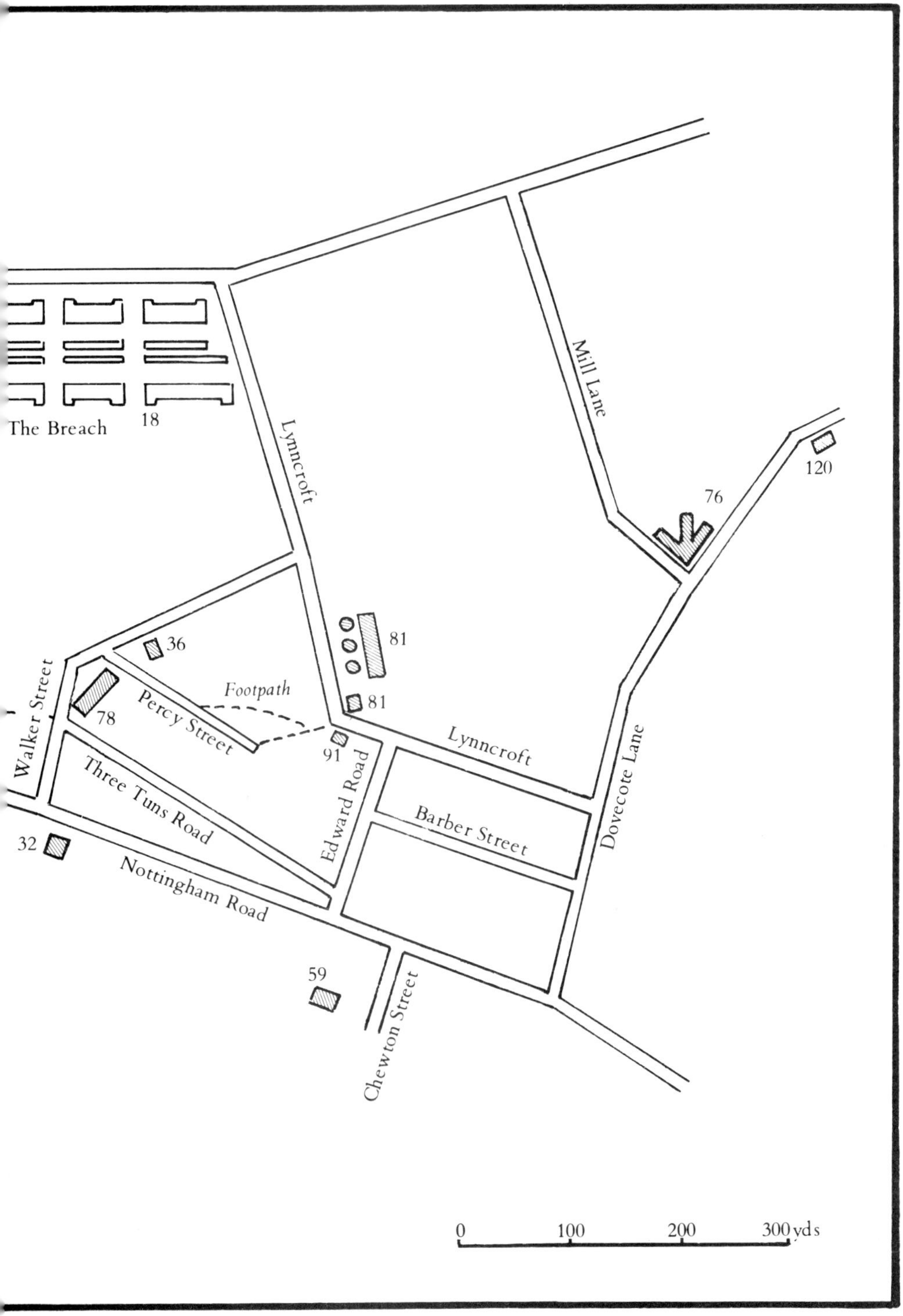
The Breach
18
Lynncroft
Mill Lane
120
76
36
81
81
Footpath
Walker Street
78
Percy Street
91
Lynncroft
Dovecote Lane
Three Tuns Road
Edward Road
Barber Street
32
Nottingham Road
59
Chewton Street
0
100
200
300 yds

14 Lamb Close, the home of the Barbers, one of Eastwood's two great mine-owning families. It appears in *The White Peacock* as Highclose, and as Shortlands in *Women in Love*.

At the end of the eighteenth century Eastwood was still a tiny settlement; by the end of the nineteenth it was a community of well over four thousand people, who had been drawn to the town directly or indirectly by the nearby mines. There had been shallow diggings in the area for centuries, but mining became a great industrial enterprise as a result of the Industrial Revolution, which generated an enormous demand for coal to drive steam engines, smelt iron, and keep a rapidly growing population warm in winter. And so in the course of the nineteenth century Eastwood developed into a prosperous market town serving the surrounding countryside and the work-force of the half a dozen nearby collieries, many of whom made their homes there. It also became a 'company town', dominated by the most important local mine-owners, Barber, Walker & Co, who were responsible for building the blocks of miners' dwellings below Nottingham Road — a public-spirited action which also gave them a double influence, as landlords as well as employers, since a collier who left their service had to leave the house he rented from them.

In typical English fashion both Barbers and Walkers used the money they made from coal to build up country estates, which meant they were not mere capitalists but also gentry — members of the traditional class of 'squires' and magistrates, still regarded as the backbone of the country. Furthermore they were able to maintain large estates very near the collieries they owned: the Walkers around their mansion at Eastwood Hall, on the Mansfield Road, between Eastwood and Brinsley, and the Barbers around Lamb Close, over to the north-east. For although industrialized, Eastwood was no urban giant like Birmingham or the pottery towns, blotting out every trace of nature. The town and the collieries were small scars on a still-lovely landscape. After a few minutes' walk down from the Nottingham Road, you could cross Beauvale Brook and go on into the lanes and paths of a valley filled with small farms and even a few patches of woodland left over from the old Sherwood Forest. The landscape stretching from Crich through Underwood and Moorgreen Reservoir to High Park Woods has become famous from Lawrence's description of it as 'the country of my heart', and from its use as a setting for episodes in *The White Peacock*, *Sons and Lovers* and other works.

So the colliers who lived on the slope between Nottingham Road and Beauvale Brook were thoroughly at home in the countryside; they walked through it every morning to work, and might even, like Arthur Lawrence, take time out to pick mushrooms or scoop up an abandoned baby rabbit. And their children — including the future novelist and poet — had a mixed inheritance that made them as familiar with flowers and streams as with ashpits and railways.

III
The Lawrences at Home

The Lawrences' first Eastwood home was in Victoria Street, one of the turnings off the Nottingham Road, not far from the market place. The little red-brick house was on the corner of an undistinguished terrace, standing upright at a sharp angle to the steeply falling road. But it was certainly nothing to be ashamed of, for although the street door opened directly on to the front room, the house itself was surprisingly roomy and substantial. The large rectangular ground-floor window gave Lydia Lawrence the idea that the front room might be turned into a shop, and for a while she displayed lace goods for sale. In the early years, with a growing family, it was evidently a struggle to make ends meet.

The clearest sign of this was the fact that one of the children had to be sacrificed. When Lydia Lawrence fell ill, George, her eldest child, spent a year at Sneinton, a working-class suburb of Nottingham, with his great-grandfather John Newton, a retired lace-factory hand in his

15 Lydia Lawrence, D.H. Lawrence's mother.

eighties who was also well known as a composer of Nonconformist hymns. And by 1887 — perhaps because Lydia was expecting yet another child — the ten or eleven-year-old George had left home for good, going to Nottingham as an apprentice picture-framer in his

16 Lawrence's birthplace on Victoria Street, Eastwood; at the time it was a corner house.

17 George Arthur Lawrence, the oldest of the Lawrence children. George lived away from home from an early age, and was a remote, though benevolent, figure to the younger members of the family, including D.H. Lawrence.

uncle's shop. He seems to have borne no grudges and to have kept in close touch with his family: at any rate he remembered his delicate brother Bert as 'a grand little lad' whom he toted about; and recalled that 'We all petted and spoiled him from the time he was born'.

As in many other families, the older Lawrence children no doubt had to look after the younger ones, and passed on the clothes they had outgrown. Sheer momentum must have taken them all down Victoria Street to play in 'the Squares'. These were prime examples of the crude, ugly buildings put up for working people in the nineteenth century, although there were still-worse places, even in Eastwood. Here were rows of mean little four-room houses, and, at the back of them, rows of box-like yards and ashpits forming squares around two large, uneven patches of earth. On these the colliers' wives hung out their washing on their clothes lines and the children played in noisy gangs.

Soon after the birth of Ada in 1887, the Lawrences moved down past the Squares to a new home. This was right on the edge of the town, in a group of eight blocks known as the Breach. Like the Squares, they were terrace houses put up by Barber, Walker & Co, but they were more recent and larger, with little gardens fronting the street, attics

18 The end house of one of the blocks making up 'the Breach' (now Garden Road) was Lawrence's home from 1887 to 1891. In *Sons and Lovers* it is 'the Bottoms'.

with dormer windows standing up from the slate roofs, and long back gardens leading down to the privy and ashpits. Among the mining folk, who were as intensely class-conscious as other Victorians, the Breach was regarded as much less 'common' than the Squares. And the Lawrences' house was a cut above the others on their row, because it

19-20 Mrs Anthony (19) and Mrs Kirk (20) were among the Lawrences' neighbours in the Breach. In *Sons and Lovers* the Breach becomes 'the Bottoms', but Lawrence left his neighbours' names unchanged. 'It was Mrs Anthony, a black-haired, strange little body, who always wore a brown velvet dress, tight-fitting.' She and 'Mrs Morel' (the character based on Mrs Lawrence) quarrelled after their sons got into a fight. Later, when Mrs Morel went into labour, she summoned Mrs Kirk, who 'climbed over the wall on to Mrs Morel's

was an end house and thè family paid sixpence a week more rent than other people — five shillings and sixpence instead of five shillings. The practical advantage of being at the end of the row was that there were three clear sides of the house with windows, letting a lot more light into the interior; and the Lawrences also had an extra strip of ground linking the front and back gardens. There was, too, a certain prestige in the different siting of the house, which stood side on against the rest of the row, with the shed-like porch set round to the left, facing the side garden.

Seen from the front, the rows making up the Breach were drab, but solid and decent. The ground-floor front room was always fitted out as a parlour, which working-class families almost never used. It contained the best furniture (often including an upright piano), smelled of polish and lack of occupation, and was occasionally opened up on some formal occasion — to entertain strangers or lay out a body before a funeral. The true sitting room, and real centre of the house, was the kitchen — despite the fact that for people in the Breach this meant sitting with a view on to the privies and ashpits, and the alley separating two rows of back gardens.

The kitchen itself was comfortable, though crowded. There was a

20

copper, and ran into her neighbour.

"Eh, dear, how are you feeling?" she cried in concern.

"You might fetch Mrs Bower," said Mrs Morel.

Mrs Kirk went into the yard, lifted up her strong, shrill voice, and called: "Aggie — Aggie!" '

large fire always going in the fireplace, for the miners got their coal cheap and it was so hot down the pit that they tended to feel the slightest draught in a room. Cooking and hot water were provided by the cast-iron kitchen range, laid out like two black filing-cabinets, one on either side of the fire. One box was the oven, the other the boiler, both heated by the fire that kept the room warm — a remarkably economical arrangement in wintertime, but inconvenient and uncomfortable in summer. Above the fire itself, at the top of the grate, stood the hob, a ledge on which food could be fried and kettles boiled. Properly speaking the whole unit, including the fire, made up the kitchen range; and all of it, including the bars of the grate, had to be black-leaded in the interests of smartness and repectability. This was one of the most laborious of all household tasks, and involved the application to the metal of a substance like boot-polish, which was brushed hard until the iron was a brilliant shining black.

21 An Eastwood barm-man; that is, an itinerant seller of yeast for baking. 'Suddenly one morning as she was looking down the alley of the Bottoms for the barm-man....' (*Sons and Lovers*).

In the Lawrences' kitchen there was a rocking chair for Mrs Lawrence on one side of the fire, and on the other side an armchair of the 'Windsor' type, with a fan pattern of spokes, reserved for her husband. There were other chairs, cupboards and dressers, a large mahogany table on which the family ate their meals, a chintz-covered sofa, and a bookcase which filled up over the years with dictionaries, the children's calf-bound prize books, and *The World's Famous Literature*, a green-bound, twenty-volume set bought by Ernest which became the family's most treasured possession. On the walls there were a few framed prints, mostly taken from magazines. The Lawrences' kitchen would probably strike us as more attractive than their neighbours' rooms, for Lydia Lawrence believed it was better to do without ornaments than to have cheap, tawdry ones. Unlike most ordinary people, who crammed their houses with knick-knacks, she was content with a pair of brass candlesticks on the mantlepiece and a vase of flowers somewhere in the room.

Just off from the kitchen was the scullery, a room hardly bigger than a cupboard, containing the cold-water tap and sink. Upstairs were the bedrooms, and above them the tiny attic. Outside the back door stood a coal-fired boiler and a water pump.

This, then, was the setting of family life in the Breach. Things were pretty much the same in all the houses the family rented. Existence was a struggle, but one that did secure the necessities, and a few cheap 'luxuries' such as paints for the children. The Lawrences and most of their neighbours were never numbered among 'the poor' — the Victorian term for the millions who always lived from hand to mouth, an entire family crowded into a single room, with no prospect but, sooner or later, ending in the workhouse. The miners' dwellings in Eastwood were unlovely, but they were adequate — not, for example, like the notoriously vile slum alleys of Sneinton, only a few miles away in Nottingham. Compared with such lost souls of the city, respectable working-class folk were well-off, especially if they lived in a tight community like mining Eastwood, with strong traditions of mutual aid. Insurance and 'the compensation' (paid by the colliery company after accidents) provided a safety-net against disaster; and even in periods of short-time working nobody starved, though on at least one occasion Mrs Lawrence, handed fourteen shillings to manage on for the week, felt that she could not go on and burst into tears.

In such times the family benefited from the fact that it was much more self-sufficient than was possible for big-city dwellers. Arthur Lawrence mended the family's shoes, kettles and pans, hung up rows of herbs in the attic for Mrs Lawrence to make into the vaguely medicinal herb beer he loved, and sometimes brought home mushrooms picked on his early morning walk to work. The children — especially little Bert and his girlfriends — scoured the countryside for blackberries so that their mother could make pies, and also gathered coltsfoot and mushrooms. Emily, the oldest girl, knitted gloves and stockings; her mother made such clothes as she could find time for. And on Friday night after dinner, Mrs Lawrence baked her own bread in the oven, leaving one of the older children to watch over it while she went shopping in the market place.

Lawrence's Eastwood

A high percentage of Lawrence's writings, including some of his best novels and short stories, are set on his native ground. These photographs indicate the persistence of the link right down to the coming of the trams in 1913, and even beyond it.

Lawrence's Eastwood. Four photographs which match his description in 'Nottingham and the Mining Countryside': 'The little market-place, with a superb outlook, ended the village on the Derbyshire side, and was just left bare, with the Sun Inn on one side, the chemist across, with the gilt pestle-and-mortar, and a shop at the other corner, and the corner of Alfreton road and Nottingham road.'

22 The market-place.

23 The chemist's shop, with mortar but no pestle. The miners bought green and yellow candles at the shop to use 'down pit'.

24 Nottingham Road from the market-place. Lawrence's 'shop at the other corner' can be seen on the far right; it was Teddy Manners' hardware store, where, it is said, miners could bring their picks to be sharpened.

23

24

MIDLAND COUNTIES BANK
BANK
MANSFIELD ROAD

25

BOOT MANUFACTURERS
Wm ALLCOCK & Co
ESTABLISHED 1854.
HOUSE FURNISHERS.
BOOT & SHOE
Wm Allcock & Co
DEPARTMENT
FURNISHING
Wm Allcock & Co
DEPARTMENT

26

25 The corner of Mansfield Road (Lawrence calls it Alfreton Road) and Nottingham Road.

26 Allcock's furniture shop. In 'Her Turn', a Lawrence short story, 'Mrs Radford went into the furnisher-and-upholsterer's shop. "There's a few things," she said to Mr Allcock, "as I'm wantin' for the house, and I might as well get them now, while the men's at home, and can shift me the furniture." '

27 During a miners' strike 'Men stood about in gangs, men were playing marbles everywhere in the streets' ('Her Turn'). Here they are playing marbles outside Goddard's store, at the corner of Lynn Croft and Edward Road, where Lawrence often shopped for his mother.

28 Moorgreen colliery — 'Minton' 'a large mine among corn fields' in *Sons and Lovers*: 'On the fallow land the young wheat shone silkily. Minton pit waved its plumes of white steam, coughed, and rattled hoarsely.'

29 The Great Northern Railway Station, Eastwood, which stood on the Derby Road. 'Paul hurried off to the station jubilant. Down Derby Road was a cherry-tree that glistened. The old brick wall by the Statutes ground burned scarlet, spring was a very flame of green' (*Sons and Lovers*).

30 The station at Kimberley, just south-east of Eastwood. It is the 'Keston' of *Sons and Lovers*, in which Paul Morel 'had to walk two and more miles from Keston home, up two long hills, down two short hills.'

31 Bunker's Hill, which appears without any change of name in *Sons and Lovers*: 'the railway ran...on to Minton, [Moorgreen: see 28] a large mine among cornfields; from Minton across the farmlands of the valleyside to Bunker's Hill, branching off there, and running north to Beggarlee and Selby, that looks over Crich and the hills of Derbyshire.'

32 Hill-Top House, Eastwood, stood almost opposite Walker Street. It was the home of the Meakin family, who broke in shire horses. So did the Pervins in Lawrence's story 'The Horse Dealer's Daughter'; their 'house was large.... At the back was a small bricked house-yard and beyond that a big square, gravelled fine and red, and having stables on two sides. Sloping, dank, winter-dark fields stretched away on the open sides.

33

34

33-6 Old Eastwood as utilized by Lawrence in his story 'The Christening'. 'The mistress of the British School stepped down from her school gate, [33; just to the right of the Congregational Chapel standing in the centre of the photograph, gable-end facing the street] and instead of turning left, as usual, she turned to the right ...She turned into Berryman's, the baker's' — Bricknall's, on Mansfield Road (34), run by Bricknall himself (35).

The mistress — Hilda Rowbotham — lived with her family in Woodbine Cottage, 'a new, substantial cottage, built with unstinted hand, such a house as an old miner could build himself out of his savings.' Woodbine Cottage in Eastwood still stands (36), proudly self-proclaimed, at the corner of Percy Street and Walker Street. The family concerned was actually named Winterbottom — as so often, Lawrence made absolutely minimal changes.

35

36

37

38

39

37-9 Three photographs which demonstrate the extraordinary fidelity with which Lawrence often transferred real scenes into his fiction. In *Sons and Lovers* Paul Morel, miserably aware that he must find a job, 'crept up the stone stairs behind the drapery shop at the Co-op', which can still be seen in the 1937 photograph (37). He went into the reading-room above the shop and looked out of the window — one of the two first-floor windows below the dormer window on the right-hand side of the photograph. 'Large sunflowers stared over the old red wall of the garden opposite'; in this photograph (38), alas, there are no sunflowers, although they did appear over the wall in season. And 'Two collieries, among the fields, waved their small white plumes of steam. Far off on the hills were the woods of Annesley, dark and fascinating'. As this photograph of 1880 shows (39), Nottingham Road was not built up on that side, so that Underwood and Moorgreen pits would have been visible, across the hedgerow, from this point.

40 Trams came to Eastwood in 1913. In his story 'Tickets, Please', set during the first World War, Lawrence describes the consequent social revolution in miniature: 'This, the most dangerous tram-service in England, as the authorities themselves declare, with pride, is entirely conducted by girls, and driven by rash young men, a little crippled, or by delicate young men, who creep forward in terror. The girls are fearless young hussies. In their ugly blue uniform, skirts up to their knees, shapeless old peaked caps on their heads, they have all the *sang-froid* of an old non-commissioned officer.'

RIPLEY
SHARMAN
SHARMAN
JEWELLERY AND CLOTHING·BARGAINS
27.29.31. HIGH St. HEANOR.
13

40

IV
Day by Day

During the years when the children were small, domestic life followed a simple, regular pattern. After the evening round of dining, washing and visiting the public house, Arthur Lawrence retired to bed. Mrs Lawrence put a big lump of coal on the fire so that it would last the night, laid out her husband's moleskin pit-trousers in front of it, and set the table for the morning. Then she turned off the gas and went to bed herself.

Mr Lawrence was up by five o'clock in the morning; everything was in readiness for him, so there was no need for his wife to get up. He got his own breakfast, and seems to have thoroughly enjoyed himself making tea and toasting bacon in front of the fire, letting the sizzling drops of fat drip down on to slices of bread. Then at dawn he went off through the fields to Brinsley colliery.

He generally arrived for work at six in the morning (unless he was on the night shift) and stayed underground until about four in the afternoon — to the envy of workers in other trades, whose hours were much longer. He lunched at his 'stall' on a couple of slices of bread and dripping and perhaps an apple; and at frequent intervals he wetted his dusty throat with cold tea from a tin bottle. Much of his life was lived by the dim light of a Davy safety lamp or, if he was certain there was no gas lingering in the mine, by the brighter light of a candle; in winter he can never have seen daylight during many a working week.

Arthur Lawrence was a skilled, responsible man. He was a 'butty', which meant that he was employed to take charge of a section of the coal-face, known as a 'stall'. When he was courting Lydia Beardsall he had described himself as a 'mining contractor'; and he appears as such on their marriage certificate. This was true — in a sense. He was paid by the week according to the amount of coal won from the stall, and he himself paid the two or three 'day men' who assisted him. As a butty he enjoyed a certain extra social standing, and could lord it a little over his day men on a Friday night, at home or in the pub, while he shared out the week's earnings. But of course he was essentially a collier among colliers, both in the world's eyes and in his own: life 'down pit' developed an intense cameraderie that mattered more than any superficial distinctions.

For miners inhabited a strange, dark, all-male world. The bad old days, when women and children toiled underground were long past, though Arthur Lawrence claimed that he had gone to work at Brinsley when he was only seven. Mining remained an essentially unmechanized industry, and winning coal from the earth still involved gangs of men hacking away at the coal face and loading the yield on to trucks, to be hauled away by horses. For hours on end Arthur Lawrence and his fellows hacked or shovelled on their knees at their low stalls, taking the whole strain of the work on their arms and shoulders. To an outsider, the dust, heat, noise and confusion added up to the conventional idea of hell, an impression intensified by the lack of space and the consciousness of being trapped beneath a mountain of rock that was only held up by a few wooden props. When the colliers came up to the surface in the 'cage', their faces were pale under their masks of coal, the result of breathing foul air for many hours. The physical strain the miner endured was visible in his overdeveloped arm and shoulder muscles, and in his dragging step at the end of the day, especially noticeable once he was past first youth.

Lydia Lawrence also had a full and exhausting day before her — and one in some respects more demoralizing than her husband's, since she was a less sociable being and kept rather aloof from the other colliers' wives. She cooked and washed up two meals a day. She mended and boiled and scrubbed and hung out the clothes of her family of six, including Arthur Lawrence's dust-caked singlets, neckerchieves and socks. She cleaned and tidied a house ravaged by children, and specked and smeared by the coal-dust that tended to find its way everywhere. And then she put on the bonnet and dark clothes she always wore, and trudged up to Nottingham Road for her shopping.

One of her main ports of call was 'the Co-op', already a great working-class institution that was particularly strong in the North and Midlands. The 'Rochdale Pioneers', a group of idealistic working men, had started the movement in 1844, opening a shop in Toad Lane, Rochdale. Business was conducted on a revolutionary but practical principle: the shop charged market prices but divided the profits among Co-op members in proportion to the amount they purchased. The movement boomed from the 'fifties, branched out into wholesaling in the 'seventies, and for a time looked like a viable general alternative to capitalism. It appealed to people like Mrs Lawrence, who had no time for Socialism — now reviving after long neglect — but believed in the virtues of hard work and self-help. And for the majority of working-class families, rarely able to save much, the dividend — 'divi' — arrived as a very useful windfall. The Lawrences used the shop so regularly that, years later, having travelled and lived in many parts of the world, Bert Lawrence wrote that he could still remember his Co-op number, 1553 A.L., better than the date of his birth.

When the shopping was done, it was probably time to start cooking again for 'the master'....There is a story that on the first day Arthur Lawrence came home from the pit to his new wife, she thought a Negro had broken into the house: she refused to believe that this man with the blackened face, red lips and brilliant white eyeballs could be her 'contractor' husband.

It's a good story, though not very convincing. Even if Arthur Lawrence had romanced a bit about his job, Lydia must have acquired some idea of mining life in advance, if only from common observation. Still, even anticipated realities can prove a shock: all at once, Lydia had been faced with a black, weary creature who hung up his pit-coat, briefly washed his hands, and slumped down before the kitchen table, waiting for his dinner. His head, shoulders and arms were still begrimed, and his thick flannel singlet was caked with pit-dust.

Lydia Lawrence found out — if she did not already know — that every collier behaved like this. They said they were too tired to wash thoroughly before they had eaten; and it was true. After dinner they expected their wives to heat water for them in a boiler and pour it into a tub or bucket. Then the miner stripped to the waist and washed himself; his wife had to scrub the coal-dust off his back — not the sort of thing a well-brought-up young lady expected to do, but since there was no other help available, she had no alternative.

In the evenings, Lydia Lawrence looked after her home and family; Arthur, if he could afford it, went out to the pub for a little while before his early bedtime. There is no evidence that he was a drunkard, or even a heavier drinker than other colliers; he was just unlucky enough to have a wife who was unwilling to put up with the colliers' way of life. They often justified their drinking on the grounds that only beer effectively washed the coal-dust from their throats. But the truth was that the pub was their social centre, a place where the cameraderie of the pit was carried on into the evening and weekends. It was a virtually all-male society (for no respectable woman would go to a public house), a working-class equivalent to the all-male clubs of the upper classes. At other times too — during fairs, short-time working and strikes — the colliers tended to stay together. They pub-crawled through the countryside to Nottingham, or took the train into the city to watch a football match; and in bad times, when they had no money and no work, they would congregate together in groups in the streets and squares of Eastwood, squatting on their heels in a peculiarly characteristic way. For long periods of time Eastwood was like a racially divided community — the men with one way of life, and the women and children with another.

Friday was a special day for the entire family: it was pay-day, and the threshold to the weekend. Miners often sent their wives or children to collect their wages at the company offices, in a big house on the Mansfield Road, roughly opposite the Barbers' home at Eastwood Hall. School even closed a few minutes early on Friday afternoon so that the children could reach the offices in time. Each of Mrs Lawrence's sons in turn performed the errand when he was old

41 The offices of Barber, Walker & Co, the mine-owners for whom Arthur Lawrence worked; as a boy, D.H. Lawrence went there every Friday afternoon to collect the wages for his father's stall. The building is still standing, on the corner of Mansfield Road and Greenhills Road.

In *Sons and Lovers* 'These offices were quite handsome: a new, red-brick building, almost like a mansion, standing in its own well-kept grounds at the end of Greenhill Lane.'

42 Alfred Brentnall, here shown in the midst of family and friends, was the cashier who paid out the miners' wages for Barber, Walker & Co on Friday afternoons. In *Sons and Lovers* the cashier is called Mr Braithwaite: 'large, somewhat of the stern patriarch in appearance, having a rather thin white beard. He was usually muffled in an enormous silk neckerchief [which can be seen in photograph 6].... Mr Braithwaite was an important share holder in the firm'.

enough, though the timid, sensitive Bert went through agonies when he was exposed to the banter of Mr Brentnall the cashier. This rough old patriarch made such an impression on him that Lawrence later put him into two novels, *Sons and Lovers* and *Aaron's Rod*.

When Arthur Lawrence had come home, eaten, washed and dressed in everyday clothes, he would divide up the week's money with his day men. If he did it at home, Mrs Lawrence would leave the kitchen, for a wife was not supposed to know what her husband earned: that way she could not complain about the size of her share. Wages were likely to

43 Alfred Wyld was Alfred Brentnall's assistant cashier; he later became chairman of Eastwood Council. Mr Braithwaite's assistant in *Sons and Lovers,* Mr Winterbottom, 'was rather small and fat, and very bald. He made remarks that were not witty, whilst his chief launched forth patriarchal admonitions against the colliers.'

vary a great deal; if a stall proved poor — hard to work, or mixed up with great lumps of rock — earnings might be very low. As a butty, Arthur Lawrence could make as much as five pounds in a really good week, though usually the sum must have been closer to two; according to D.H. Lawrence, his father's earnings actually fell over the years because he antagonized his superiors and was consistently given bad stalls. Still, Mrs Lawrence seems to have received an average of about thirty shillings a week for housekeeping, from which she paid the rent, trade union dues that Arthur would probably have been too careless to deal with regularly, and 'clubs' and other forms of welfare payment. Ironically, the various benefit payments, made when Mr Lawrence was in hospital as a result of an accident at the pit, often amounted to more than a normal week's housekeeping; so that the family hoped he would get better — but not too soon.

On most Friday nights, when Mrs Lawrence wandered among the covered stalls in front of the Sun Inn, she had ninepence or a shilling to spend on extras — a little bit of lace, a pretty dish or a few flowers. The tiny market place was thronged with women looking over goods and haggling; others crossed the road and stared at the fine clothes in

44-5 Eastwood Market. 'Mrs Morel loved her marketing. In the tiny market-place on the top of the hill, where four roads, from Nottingham and Derby, Ilkeston and Mansfield, meet, many stalls were erected.' (*Sons and Lovers*) A different view of the market-place (45) shows the Sun Inn and, on the far left, a billboard leaning against the croft wall of the inn; it advertises the current programme of Parker's cinema (see photograph 68), which stood in the croft.

44

45

46

46 Eastwood's Congregational Chapel, built in 1867-8; it served as a landmark for travellers approaching the town from the north and west. During Robert Reid's ministry the 'Congo' became the centre of Eastwood's intellectual life, and as such was an important influence on the young Lawrence.

the windows of London House, George Henry Cullen's drapery store — clothes so absurdly out of place in Eastwood that the dandyish, ever-sanguine Cullen would eventually be forced to sell them for a fraction of their value. Over the years Cullen leased one section after another of London House to more successful shopkeepers, but his taste for lost-cause business ventures remained strong, providing D.H. Lawrence with some of the more entertaining material for *The Lost Girl*.

The town was most alive early on Friday evening. The streets were full of men on their way to the pub, the billiard hall, or a sixpenny 'hop'; if they were not driven by the urgencies of courting they might linger for a while and give ear to an orator who had set up his soap-box near the market.

By eleven o'clock it was all over. The stalls had closed and the women had gone long before; all the respectable girls had reluctantly left their young men, or were just arriving home to a motherly scolding about the dangers of late-night passion and men inflamed with drink; the men themselves were walking, reeling or crawling on their way.

Saturday was less ritualized. For wives, of course, it was another working day, complicated by having the children home from school. And the house had to be kept spick and span over the weekend, ready to receive callers. It was a day for excursions and visits, though for husbands it might also be one for long sessions at the pub, depending on finances and relations at home.

Sunday was different from every other day: it was dedicated almost

47 'The Primitive Methodist Chapel is a big barn of a place, built, designed, and paid for by the colliers themselves. But it threatened to fall down from its first form, so that a professional architect had to be hired at last to pull the place together.' Lawrence's description in the story 'Strike Pay' is correct in all particulars. The Chapel in Eastwood's 'Squares' *was* declared unsafe, and the roof had to be lowered; the original front gable end was retained, as the photograph shows.

48 Strikers leaving the Primitive Methodist Chapel in the 1920s. 'Strike-money is paid in the Primitive Methodist Chapel. The crier was round quite early on Wednesday morning to say that paying would begin at ten o'clock.' ('Strike Pay')

entirely to rest and religion. Mrs Lawrence took her children morning and evening to the Congregational Chapel on the corner of the Nottingham Road and Albert Street, one turning down from Victoria Street. The children went to Sunday School at the chapel as well, joined the Young People's Society of Christian Endeavour, and spent one evening a week at the anti-liquor Band of Hope, where they solemnly signed the abstainers' pledge and roared out 'There's a serpent in the glass, dash it down!' and other rousing songs. Mr Lawrence rarely attended chapel (though he made a good impression when he did), presumably finding small comfort in the temperance propaganda and rather self-consciously 'intellectual' atmosphere.

It was probably just this atmosphere that attracted Lydia Lawrence. She would scarcely have been happy at the highly emotional, hell-and-damnation meetings of the Primitive Methodists, though many colliers were 'Prim Ranters' and their chapel on the Squares had largely been built by their efforts. By contrast with the Methodists and Baptists, Congregationalism had acquired a genteel aura by the nineteenth century, combined with a reserved fervour that appealed to respectable but hard-working people such as shopkeepers and smallholders. The chapel itself, irreverently nicknamed 'the Congo', dated from 1868 and

49 Harvest Festival at Eastwood Congregational Church. 'I liked our chapel, which was tall and full of light, and yet still; and colour-washed pale green and blue, with a bit of lotus pattern. And over the organ loft, "O worship the Lord in the beauty of holiness", in big letters.' ('Hymns in a Man's Life')

was built in the Neo-Gothic style used for so many Victorian buildings — an imitation of the style of the great medieval cathedrals, even to the tall spire. Inside, the chapel was light and spacious, with blue and green decorations and a large organ and loft with 'Worship the Lord in the beauty of holiness' inscribed round the arch in front of it.

Instead of hell-fire, the congregation was usually treated to a sermon more like a lecture — perhaps even too 'reasonable' and undogmatic for some of its hearers, since the ministers were university men who did not always believe in the literal truth of Scripture. However, Mrs Lawrence evidently enjoyed the intellectual atmosphere, and later she also joined the literary society started by Robert Reid, the young Scottish minister appointed in 1897. Both the minister and the Sunday School superintendant, Mr Remington, seem to have preferred martial rather than mournful hymns, and Bert Lawrence never failed to be stirred by 'Sound the Battle-Cry' and 'Stand Up, Stand Up for Jesus'. Mrs Lawrence cultivated the minister and used to invite him to tea. But the genteel nature of the occasion was likely to be marred by the arrival of Arthur Lawrence from the pit, ready either to reproach the minister with his clean hands and exemption from toil, or to appeal for his pity with a description of the collier's hard life.

50 The Reverend Robert Reid, minister of Eastwood Congregational Church from 1898 to 1911. In *Sons and Lovers* the minister is Mr Heaton, who 'was young, and very poor. His wife had died at the birth of his first baby, so he remained alone in the manse. He was a Bachelor of Arts of Cambridge, very shy, and no preacher.'

There were other local occasions that arrived less frequently but with equal regularity — Christmas, and Harvest Festival, and the twice-yearly water-parties given by the Barbers on the shores of Moorgreen Reservoir. These were gay, elegant affairs to which the miners and their wives were invited, though they were segregated from the grander guests; Lawrence has described it all brilliantly in *Women in Love*, where the water-party becomes the setting for a double drowning based on the Barber tragedy (which in reality occurred at a private birthday party).

Twice a year the entire population of Eastwood went to the local fairs. The first, in September, was the Hill Top Wakes, held at the eastern end of the town, outside the Three Tuns Inn; then, in November, there was the Statutes and Fair on the other side of Eastwood, just down from the market place. The merry-go-rounds, coconut shies, shooting galleries and games were much the same as they are in modern fairs; only the peepshows, and real or reported marvels such as bearded ladies, are no longer seen. As it grew darker,

51-2 Mr and Mrs Thomas Barber. The Barber family owned five pits in the Eastwood area, employing over 3,000 men and boys. D.H. Lawrence's father worked at one of the Barber pits, Brinsley, and Lawrence himself seems to have been fascinated by the family. His novel *Women in Love* describes or refers to several incidents in the Barbers' history, notably the accident in which their son Philip shot his brother, and the drowning of his sister in Moorgreen Reservoir.

53 The company of Teddy Rayner's 'twopenny travelling theatre', which regularly visited Eastwood, performing in a big tent in the Sun Inn croft. Watching a company of Italian strolling players performing 'Amleto', Lawrence recalled seeing *Hamlet* in Rayner's 'Blood-Tub' as a child; his description suggests that neither the artistes nor the spectators were well grounded in Shakespearean studies.

the ground would be dramatically lit by naphtha (oil) flares for the customers, who by that time consisted chiefly of young men and women. The small boys would linger as long as they dared, though they had probably spent their twopences—halfpenny by halfpenny—during the early afternoon. Many of the men would have retired to the pub, and Arthur Lawrence's favourite, the Three Tuns, would be so packed that he would probably offer to help serve drinks there in return for some beer and pocket money.

Also very popular were the strolling players, who often took in Eastwood on their tours. The best known, Teddy Rayner's company, set up a big tent ('The Blood Tub') and in good times might stay for months, harrowing their audiences at twopence a head with famous melodramas such as *Sweeney Todd, the Demon Barber of Fleet Street* and *Maria Marten, or Murder in the Red Barn*. The style of acting would have been as gruesome and exaggerated as the plots and dialogue; and the same kind of treatment was meted out to more exalted works. In *Twilight in Italy* Lawrence remembered being thrilled as a child by a performance of *Hamlet* in which the Ghost cried out ' 'Amblet, 'Amblet, I *am* thy father's ghost.' Such as it was, the effect was spoiled by a voice from the audience: 'Why tha arena, I can tell thy voice.'

When there were no professionals to entertain them, the more enterprising inhabitants of Eastwood put on 'penny readings' at the British School on Albert Street, next to the 'Congo'. These consisted of musical or comic turns by local people, culminating in one of the most popular of all Victorian entertainments —a dramatic reading in the style of Dickens, which thus survived into the age of the cinema.

Picture Essay

Fact into Fiction: 'THE LOST GIRL'

Of all Lawrence's novels after the autobiographical *Sons and Lovers, The Lost Girl* is the closest to conventionally realistic fiction. In it Lawrence paints a convincing picture of provincial society in 'Woodhouse' and describes the careers of James Houghton and his daughter Alvina. The first half of Lawrence's novel was in fact not merely realistic: it was authentic. James, Alvina and the other members of the Houghton household were easily recognizable as — perhaps even hard to distinguish from — the Cullens of Eastwood.

54 Nottingham Road. In the top right-hand corner of the photograph are the windows of 'Co-op Hall', where (in *Sons and Lovers*) 'When the children were old enough to be left, Mrs Morel joined the Women's Guild.'

George Henry Cullen's shop, London House, can be seen on the left, beneath the arched windows. Cullen was the original of James Houghton in *The Lost Girl*, and 'Manchester House' was 'a vast square building — vast, that is, for Woodhouse — standing on the main street and high-road of the small but growing town. The lower front consisted of two fine shops, one for Manchester goods, one for silk and woollens. This was James Houghton's commercial poem.'

Cullen, like James Houghton, found himself obliged to lease half of the building — a development already visible in the photograph. 'Carpenters and joiners appeared, and the premises were completely severed.' In reality, Cullen's lessee was a grocer; in the novel, Houghton's failure is emphasized by making the newcomer a competitor — a successful 'parvenu' haberdasher.

55 This photograph, taken after Cullen's time, shows the final state of London House, with Cullen's shop occupying no more than a third of the original frontage —just as Houghton's drapery business did in *The Lost Girl*.

56 Miss Fanny Wright, the governess, was the prop of the Cullen household. Her counterpart in *The Lost Girl* is Miss Frost, 'a handsome, vigorous young woman of about thirty years of age, with grey-white hair and gold-rimmed spectacles. The white hair was not at all tragical: it was a family trait.'

57 A verse from Wordsworth copied by Miss Wright.

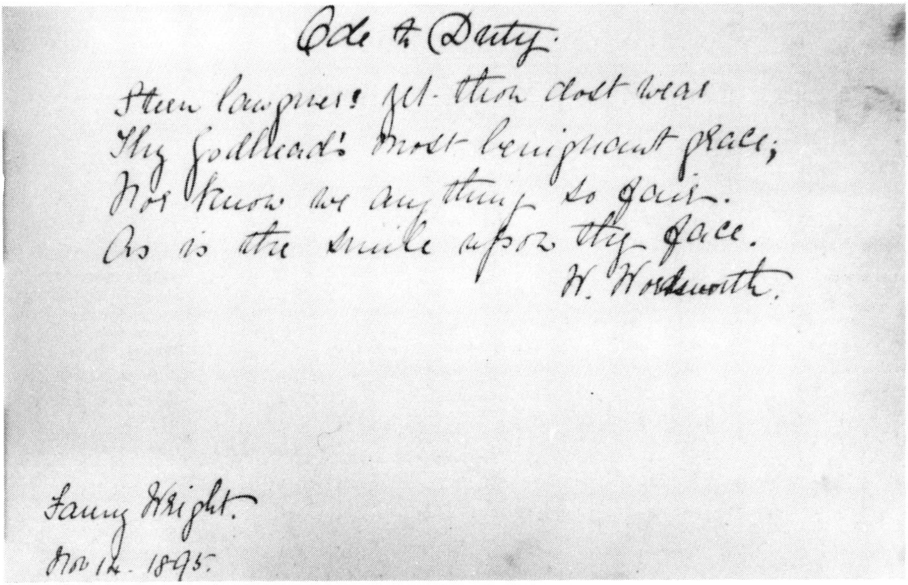

Ode to Duty.

Stern Lawgiver! yet thou dost wear
Thy Godhead's most benignant grace;
Nor know we anything so fair
As is the smile upon thy face.
W. Wordsworth.

Fanny Wright.
Nov 12. 1895.

58 Flossie (Florence) Cullen, George Henry Cullen's daughter, was the inspiration for Alvina Houghton in *The Lost Girl*: 'She grew up a slim girl, rather distinguished in appearance, with a fine, slightly arched nose, and beautiful grey-blue eyes over which the lids tilted with a very odd, sardonic tilt.' Alvina, like Flossie, 'never went to school. She had her lessons from her beloved governess.'

59

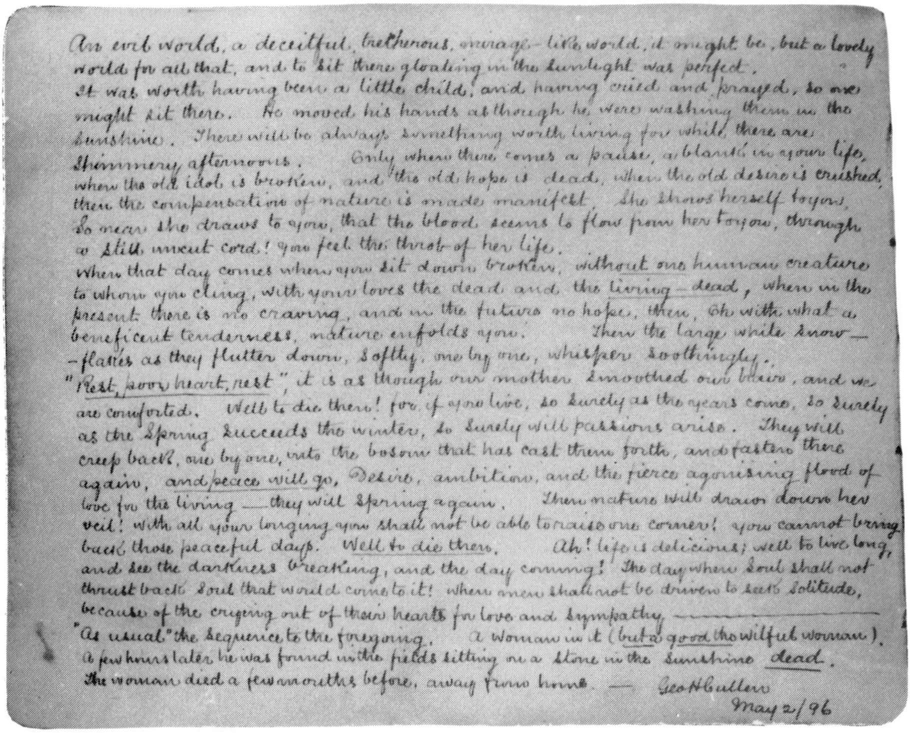

An evil world, a deceitful, treacherous, mirage-like world, it might be, but a lovely world for all that, and to sit there gloating in the sunlight was perfect.
It was worth having been a little child, and having cried and prayed, so one might sit there. He moved his hands as though he were washing them in the sunshine. There will be always something worth living for while there are shimmery afternoons. Only when there comes a pause, a blank in your life, when the old idol is broken, and the old hope is dead, when the old desire is crushed, then the compensation of nature is made manifest. She shows herself to you, so near she draws to you, that the blood seems to flow from her to you, through a still uncut cord! you feel the throb of her life.
When that day comes when you sit down broken, without one human creature to whom you cling, with your loves the dead and the living-dead, when in the present there is no craving, and in the future no hope, then, Oh with what a beneficent tenderness, nature enfolds you. Then the large white snow-flakes as they flutter down, softly, one by one, whisper soothingly.
"Rest, poor heart, rest", it is as though our mother smoothed our brow, and we are comforted. Well to die then! for if you live, so surely as the years come, so surely as the Spring succeeds the winter, so surely will passions arise. They will creep back, one by one, into the bosom that has cast them forth, and fasten there again, and peace will go, Desire, ambition, and the fierce agonising flood of love for the living — they will spring again. Then nature will draw down her veil! with all your longing you shall not be able to raise one corner! you cannot bring back those peaceful days. Well to die then. Ah! life is delicious; well to live long, and see the darkness breaking, and the day coming! The day when soul shall not thrust back soul that would come to it! when men shall not be driven to seek solitude, because of the crying out of their hearts for love and sympathy ————
"As usual" the sequence to the foregoing. A Woman in it (but a good tho wilful woman).
A few hours later he was found in the fields sitting on a stone in the sunshine dead.
The woman died a few months before, away from home. — Geo H Cullen
May 2/96

60

59 There appears to be no surviving photograph of George Henry Cullen, one of Eastwood's more remarkable characters — evidently a man of a restless, imaginative turn that found expression in wildly impractical 'commercial poems'. Like James Houghton in *The Lost Girl*, he tried to make money out of a little windlass pit that produced cheap, inferior coal; both the real and the fictional pits were called 'Throttle-Ha'penny'. The photograph shows Throttle-Ha'penny Engine House, after it had evidently closed down, since the aperture through which the winding ropes ran has been bricked up.

60 Like 'James, whose prayers were beautiful', Cullen was a leading Congregationalist. A strange prayer that he composed has a few almost Lawrentian turns of phrase.

61 George Henry Cullen's wife Lucy was an invalid like Mrs Houghton in *The Lost Girl*: 'the invalid ... mostly sat, in her black dress with a white lace collar fastened by a twisted gold brooch, in her room, doing nothing, nervous and heart-suffering'.

62 The Miners' Welfare was formerly the Mechanics' Institute; the Lawrences borrowed books from the institute's library on a Thursday afternoon. In their day the premises of the Eastwood Conservative Club were next door, on the ground and first floors. Surprisingly, D.H. Lawrence's miner father, Arthur Lawrence, was a member. So were George Henry Cullen and his fictional counterpart, James Houghton: 'The shop was now only opened on Friday afternoons and evenings, so every day, twice a day, James was seen dithering bareheaded and hastily down the street, as if pressed by fate, to the Conservative Club.' In *The Lost Girl* it is described as 'that degenerated and shabby, down-at-heel club.'

63-4 Dr Duncan McDonald Forbes, an Eastwood GP who married into the Barber family. He evidently suggested Dr Fordham in *The Lost Girl*, who is consulted when Alvina proposes to become a nurse: 'Dr Fordham didn't approve, certainly he didn't — but neither did he see any great harm in it.'

65 Flossie Cullen in nursing uniform. In *The Lost Girl* Alvina's choice of career is related to the lack of eligible men in Eastwood: 'At that time it was rather the thing for young ladies to enter the nursing profession, if their hopes had been blighted or checked in another direction!.... Instead of a trousseau, nurse's uniforms in fine blue-and-white stripe, with great white aprons. Instead of a wreath of orange blossom, a rather chic nurse's bonnet of blue silk, and for a trailing veil, a blue silk fall.'

67 Langley Mill, a village about a mile from Eastwood. The last of George Henry Cullen's ventures was a cinema, erected next to the kiosk on the right-hand side of this photograph. In *The Lost Girl* 'James was inoculated with the idea of starting a cinema on the virgin soil of Lumley.'

In the centre, in the distance, stands Langley Mill Co-operative, where Ernest Lawrence took his first job at the age of thirteen.

66 The Eastwood Empire, built in 1913 by F.G. Stubbs. Its existence may have persuaded George Henry Cullen to try his luck outside Eastwood. This was certainly the reasoning of his fictional counterpart, James Houghton: 'Woodhouse had a cinema already: a famous Empire run-up by Jordan, the sly builder and decorator.'

67

68 Parker's cinema in Eastwood suggested Wright's in *The Lost Girl*, which James Houghton's partner visited. 'Mr May's mind, though quick, was pedestrian, not winged. He had come to Woodhouse not to look at Jordan's "Empire", but at the temporary wooden structure that stood in the old Cattle Market — "Wright's Cinematograph and Variety Theatre". Wright's was not a superior show, like the Woodhouse Empire. Yet it was always packed with colliers and work-lasses.'

69 Flossie Cullen with her husband, George Hodgkinson, and her son William; she died about three years after this photograph was taken. George Hodgkinson worked in the pay-box of Cullen's cinema. He was understandably angry at Lawrence's use of Flossie's personal history in *The Lost Girl*, although the later life of Lawrence's heroine, Alvina Houghton, is quite different from Flossie's: Alvina joins a theatrical troupe and eventually marries an Italian!

The locket Flossie is wearing here contained the photographs of her mother and Fanny Wright which are reproduced in this book (56 and 61).

69

V
Growing

Early childhood in Eastwood must have been quite exciting. There were the shops and squares and claypits of the town; the black-faced miners climbing the hill from the pit; and the colliery itself, with shooting steam and clanking trucks of coal, gradually fading away until, after dark, nothing was left but a pattern of lights down the valley. And there was the countryside, stretching out in a vista of lanes, paths, hedges and fields from Beauvale Brook, hardly any distance from the Breach.

Bert Lawrence and his brothers and sisters got to know the countryside well, for they regularly walked across the fields to visit their grandparents in Brinsley. These were Arthur Lawrence's father and mother, John and Sarah Lawrence. John was a tailor employed by Barber, Walker & Co; until the 1890s the company supplied all the colliers' pit clothes, so there was regular work for the old man. To Bert, great rolls of material, stacked up in the workshop, were a familiar sight — especially flannel, used for singlets and as a lining for pit-trousers; and there was a big, strange-looking old sewing machine used in making the tough, heavy trousers. Some time in the 'nineties John Lawrence retired to a little cottage near the pit; the children continued to visit him there, and also saw three sets of aunts and uncles on the Lawrence side of the family, all held at Brinsley in the grip of the mine.

There was plenty to do closer to home. Naturally, forbidden places in the town exercised a fatal attraction. One such was the clay pits, ruled by a mysterious character the children called Mako Koko, who made and handed out a kind of toffee which they consumed while feeling half-afraid that it might poison them.

But in summer the brook called: there were places in it where you could swim, and just across the sheep-bridge you could see the sheep being sheared, or veer towards the pavilion of the cricket field which the colliery company provided for their men. A favourite game was to crawl under the pavilion, which was raised a foot or so above the ground on wooden blocks. The boys who were brave enough to crawl the length of the pavilion were hailed as good potential colliers by their friends, for most Eastwood boys thought it would be the finest thing in the world to follow their fathers' occupation.

Lydia Lawrence thought otherwise. In the ordinary course of things her sons would have gone down the pit and her daughters into domestic service, at least until they got married. But, having been disappointed in her own life, Mrs Lawrence was determined to do better than that for her children, and she visualised the boys in 'white collar' jobs which never involved getting dirty, such as clerking, teaching, or even the Congregational ministry. Most ambitious parents felt the same way, for although a clerk might not always earn as much as some manual workers, he could hope for promotion and was less likely to find himself unemployed; and he did not share the manual worker's fear that his earnings would fall drastically as his physical strength declined with middle and old age. Even Arthur Lawrence must have realised something of this, for although he resented the implied slight on mining, he never seriously opposed his wife's plans to keep her sons out of the pit.

One worldly advantage Mrs Lawrence gave her children was the ability to speak a standard, dialect-free English. Once, the young Arthur Lawrence's caressing 'thees' and 'thous' had charmed her; but she soon came to see them only as a sign of 'commonness', telling all the world that their user belonged to the 'lower classes'. Her husband's insults when they quarrelled — he called her a 'sliving bitch' or told her to 'hoad the faece' (shut up) — understandably strengthened her prejudices. She used to claim that she had never been able to imitate the local speech, but the way she brought up her children revealed her true feelings: they were never allowed to use dialect within her hearing. The result was that they actually grew up handily 'bi-lingual', since they employed dialect freely outside the house.

Mrs Lawrence was only able to make ambitious plans for them because there were greater opportunities for working-class children than in the past. Arthur Lawrence had done well enough to become barely literate as a result of attending a few classes held by a Miss Eite at Brinsley; his children were given several years' education by order of the state and largely at its expense. The Education Act of 1870 made a real division between generations of Eastwood families, just as it made a division between generations all over the country. The Act laid down that every child must have an 'elementary education', and one after another the Lawrence children duly attended Beauvale Board School, a large, red-brick, bell-towered institution on the eastern edge of the town.

Ernest, the Lawrences' second son, was a splendid scholar — so much so that even years later the headmaster held him up as an example to his youngest brother and sister. In fact Ernest was one of those marvellously gifted young people who so often seem to burn

70 The able, hard-working Ernest Lawrence, older brother of D.H.L., seemed certain to make his mark in the business world while still a young man.

themselves out or die young. He had almost every imaginable good quality: he was clever, popular and athletic, and so full of vitality that he always leapt a fence rather than climb over it or go through a gate. He was good company, with a jocular nickname for every member of the family (Emily was 'Injun Topknot' because of her hairstyle, Bert 'Billy White-Nob' or 'William Whytteun') and a fund of boisterous humour; on one occasion, when Bert and Ada were dolefully burying a dead rabbit, Ernest suddenly appeared in a black silk hat with mourning streamers, lamenting with such noisy insincerity that the children's distress dissolved in laughter.

As if all this was not enough, Ernest was intensely ambitious and hard-working. He left school at twelve and held a series of clerical jobs while he learned shorthand and typing at evening classes; later still he took correspondence courses in Business French and German. His progress was so good that, when he was still only twenty-one, he was offered a job in the office of a London shipping underwriter, John Holroyd & Co of Lime Street. It was a magnificent opportunity for a boy from an obscure little mining town.

Mrs Lawrence was torn between pride and possessiveness, and only

71-2 Ernest Lawrence, possibly in the Walker Street house; and Ernest, centre, with friends. Unlike the formal portraits, these photographs convey the vitality and charm that made Ernest a family favourite. His premature death in October 1901 was a crucial event in the family's history and D.H. Lawrence's life: partly, at least, as a result, Lawrence became ill, replaced Ernest in his mother's affections, and was liberated from his job in Haywood's surgical goods factory.

73

73 Ernest Lawrence with his fiancée, the darkly handsome Gypsy Dennis. Ernest's family seem to have thought her a shallow, flighty creature who encouraged him to spend too much money — which may or may not have been true; the reaction of the Lawrences, a puritanical, provincial and close-knit family group, is not very good evidence. In *Sons and Lovers* 'William was succeeding with his "Gipsy", as he called her.... her name was Louisa Lily Denys Weston.'

74 Gypsy Dennis

let Ernest go with a certain bitterness: she wanted her children to be successes, but somehow to manage it while staying by her side. Ernest had become the first of her 'lovers': she had frightened off the girls he met at dances when they came calling; and later, when he took a job at Coventry, he had cycled dutifully home every weekend. But after he left for London, Ernest began to show signs of growing up. As a bachelor earning the princely sum of thirty shillings a week, he could afford to send money home to keep his mother in smart gloves and boots. But without Mrs Lawrence there to interfere, he soon became engaged to a pretty, well-bred girl — one of the new breed of female office workers. The girl, Gypsy Dennis, was a gay little creature who enjoyed party-going and was willing enough to let Ernest spend his hard-earned money on her, though it is now impossible to say whether she was as shallow as the implacably biased Lawrence family believed.

In spite of his new entanglement, Ernest remained the family favourite, and he was received with rapture whenever he visited Eastwood, bearing crystallized fruits and other exotic presents. Now he would sometimes parade up and down the main street in his frock

75 Emily Una Lawrence, D.H. Lawrence's older sister, as a young woman.

coat and silk hat; the colliers sneered at him (and no doubt felt twinges of envy too), but Ernest's family looked on in awe, accepting him as the very model of a gentleman. None of them doubted that he would make a great career for himself, or that he and no other was the genius of the family.

And certainly the older girl, Emily, gradually settled from being a tomboy into a placid, conventional young woman. But Bert, the youngest boy, also showed promise, though lacking Ernest's apparent rude health and drive. Despite his mother's fears Bert had survived babyhood, but he grew into a painfully thin little boy, weighing so little that his brother George could carry him across the fields for hours on end without effort. He remained weak-chested and utterly incapable of joining in rough street games or competitive sports, and most of his early boyhood was spent in the company of girls, whom he loved to organize for blackberrying expeditions. He was shy and over-sensitive too, crying so readily that even protective little friends such as Mabel Thurlby grew exasperated and told him to shut up. But in the right company he could be full of life and fun. He brought a strange, passionate attention to everything he saw or did, and people noticed his peculiarly fine, quick reaction to persons, plants and animals. Inevitably, Emily was a second mother to him, and the rest of the family spoiled him. And he was so obviously frail that most adults were kind to him, although a few rough but harmless remarks might be enough to persuade him that he was being tormented past all bearing. Strangely enough, he enjoyed doing household jobs, and by the time he was ten could often be found with a big apron draped round him, cleaning knives and forks, polishing the family's boots, scrubbing the floor, or even blackleading the kitchen range. These were unusual occupations for even a frail boy at a time and place when no male — even if unemployed — would condescend to do 'women's work'.

Many boys were less tolerant of Bert Lawrence than grown-ups and girls. At the Board School he was looked on as a 'mardarse' or cissy — weak, a bit stuck-up, and odd (for he preferred girls to boys, and did a good deal of painting). Any boy could hit him without fear of

76 Beauvale Boys' School, where D.H. Lawrence received his elementary education. This old photograph shows the school's imposing bell tower, which was taken down in 1926.

retaliation, and so he was branded a coward. At one time a gang of lads from the Breach used to chant

Dicky Dicky Denches
Plays with the wenches

when they saw him with the girls; and he was small and sensitive enough to be hurt by the rather feeble jibe. A few years later, in his teens, he was already so quick and verbally adept that he could give better than he got, making the other colliers' sons smart under his sarcasms. However, such hostility seems never to have gone very deep, perhaps because Bert was too frail, and led too home-centred a life, for fighting or bullying or similar involvements.

Given Lydia Lawrence's ambitions for her children, school work

77 Lawrence's class at Beauvale Boys' School, 1894. The teacher is 'Nocker' Bradley, a fierce boy-tamer. Lawrence is the second boy from the left in the third row from the top; his long-time friend George Henry Neville ('Diddler') is sitting immediately below him. The influence of locality on Lawrence is indicated by the way in which so many of the boys's names — Birkin, Burrows, Braithwaite, Meakin, Thurlby —figure in his life and/or work.

was a more serious worry. Bert was clever, but not much interested in the dull rote learning drilled into the boys at the Board School; and studying gave him headaches. The school itself was a surprisingly big, airy place, but the classes were very large, and it was by no means uncommon for several sets of sixty pupils to occupy the same room while each worked on a different lesson. Discipline was harsh; at Beauvale the headmaster, W.W. Whitehead, used the cane freely to compel the respect and attention of the unruly colliers' sons. It was Mrs Lawrence who drove Bert on, sharing his tasks and probably encouraging him to be like his big brother Ernest, of whom Bert felt a sort of affectionate jealousy. 'Gaffer' Whitehead also helped, though at their first encounter he had been outraged by Bert's stubborn refusal to answer to his first name, David, which the headmaster seems to have taken as some kind of slight on the King David of the Old Testament. Lawrence won his point, however, as the headmaster's logbook shows: he appears in it as variously 'Lawrence B.', 'Herbert D. Lawrence' and — in 1898, triumphant winner of the County Council scholarship for which Whitehead had coached him — 'Herbert David Lawrence'. Only retrospectively, in the prize list, did Whitehead get the names in the right order, crediting 'D. Herbert Lawrence'.

Lawrence's County Council scholarship was worth twelve pounds a year for three years. He was the first Eastwood boy to win such an award, and now became one of the privileged minority in England who went on to receive a secondary education. (The first state legislation on the subject was not passed until 1902.) In September 1898, when he was just thirteen, he enrolled as a pupil at Nottingham High School, an ancient, highly respectable institution where the masters were university men and sported mortar boards, and where Bert had to wear the standard uniform of blue cap and knickerbockers.

It was a real sacrifice to send him there. The scholarship meant three more years of supporting him, and for Mrs Lawrence three more years of skimping and saving. The twelve pounds covered only part of the cost of Bert's clothing, train fares, dinners and books; Mrs Lawrence complained bitterly and gave out that she had doubts, but it was probably certain from the very beginning that she would let him go.

Nor was it easy for Bert himself. He had to leave home at seven in the morning, rush to catch a train to Nottingham's Victoria Station, and then climb a hill to the school, arriving towards the end of Assembly. And by the time he got back home it was seven in the evening and there was still homework to be done. It would have been exhausting for a more robust boy, and not surprisingly Bert developed a little cough he never afterwards got rid of.

This may account for the way his career at the High School tailed off. For a time he was outstandingly good at French, German and writing, and later on he won prizes for mathematics; but by the final year his position was fifteenth out of a class of nineteen.

Mr and Mrs Lawrence must have wondered at this stage whether it had been worth the sacrifices. Bert had not even made any friends or useful contacts at school. As the only collier's son in a middle-class institution that tried to create a 'public school' atmosphere, he may have felt rather out of place; and on one occasion the parents of a friend stopped the boys meeting when they discovered Bert's background. In any case, the long daily journeys to and from Nottingham must have made out-of-school friendships hard to develop. It is a curious fact that Lawrence, so copious and so autobiographical as a writer, has virtually nothing to say of his schooldays, whether under Whitehead or at Nottingham High.

It was now decided that Bert, having had the luxury of three extra years' education, should follow the same path as his brother Ernest and find employment as a clerk. When an advertisement appeared in the *Nottinghamshire Guardian*, offering a clerical position in a firm making surgical goods, Bert answered it. His application was mainly the work of Ernest Lawrence, who was home on a visit and knew all there was to know about business letters. There is an element of retrospective comedy in the great D.H. Lawrence being solemnly directed to put down the banalities admired as good business style: 'Should you favour me with the appointment I would always endeavour to merit the confidence you place in me', and so on. But in this matter Ernest really did know best: Bert got the job and went to work for Haywood's of Castle Gate in Nottingham.

At last he too was making a contribution to the family budget: thirteen shillings a week. For this he worked six full days every week, starting at eight in the morning and finishing at eight almost every night — after which he had a train journey and a two-mile walk home. It was some compensation that the working day at Haywood's was a peaceful, leisurely affair. The main drawback was the factory girls — a rough lot who embarrassed Bert by bombarding him with suggestive remarks, and on one occasion cornered him and tried to tear off his trousers.

But there he was, spending his day perched on a high stool, translating letters from foreign customers and copying orders into a big book. This, it must have seemed certain, was to be the kind of thing he would do for the rest of his working life.

VI
Life at Walker Street

Meanwhile the Lawrences had left the Breach. In 1891 they moved further up the hill to Walker Street, from which they had a splendid view of the valley across the waste ground and clay-pits; but the exposed position of the house made it vulnerable to the cold north wind, and Bert nicknamed it 'Bleak House', after the novel by Dickens.

The new home was socially superior to the house in the Breach; it was one of a block that had just been built, and it had a bay window — a matter of considerable prestige in those days. It was probably no coincidence that Ernest had just left school and gone to work, so that he had become a contributor instead of a dependant. The difference was a vital one, and the best years for many working-class families were those in which the children were employed and bringing in money, before they married and set up homes of their own. In a sense, Mrs Lawrence had a straightforward economic grievance against Gypsy Dennis, whose fascinations had the effect of diverting resources from the family.

But of course Lydia Lawrence would have hated any girl who threatened her hold on her beloved sons; within a few years she was showing a similar hostility to Bert's girlfriends. And she did nothing to stop all the children taking her side in quarrels with Arthur Lawrence, whom they learned to hate and despise. As a child, Bert told Mabel Thurlby that he loved only his mother, though some older contemporaries remembered a time when he and the other children greeted their father with joy when he got home, hanging round his neck and getting themselves covered in coal dust. As a young man Bert certainly came to loathe his father so intensely that Arthur Lawrence's presence in the room often killed the life in him and left him in a state of malignant sulks. Years afterwards, when it was too late, both Bert and Ada came to see that there were two sides to the quarrels, and that their mother had done wrong in turning them so completely against their father.

Arthur Lawrence certainly seemed nothing like an ogre to outsiders. Many years later, one Eastwood fellow-worker characterized him as 'always a perfect gentleman'; and May Chambers, the girl who noted the ugly transformation he caused in Bert, also wrote that, at the moment when it occurred, Arthur Lawrence was chatting with her in a completely normal fashion. He was even normal enough to be proud of his ladylike wife and his clever children who knew French — though, naturally, when they were ranged against him he would disparage both ladylike airs and book learning.

There were still times when the conflicts were forgotten. Arthur Lawrence was at his best when he was active, and the children enjoyed it when he was cobbling or mending. He would sit on the floor in front of the hearth, his legs crossed tailor-fashion, and hammer away, sing, and send the children scampering about to fetch tools and materials. In

78 Walker Street, where the Lawrence family lived from 1891. They are generally supposed to have moved to Lynn Croft in 1904, but George Hardy points out that the *Eastwood and Kimberley Advertiser* of 10 March 1905 congratulates 'Mr D.H. Lawrence of Walker Street' on his success in the King's Scholarship Examination; so it looks as though the move must have taken place then or later.

There is some question as to which of the Walker Street houses was the Lawrences' home, known at the time as No 3. The street originated as a block of seven houses built by the Mellor family, and everything depends on which way the old numbers ran: if from the Nottingham Road end, then the present No 8 Walker Street was the Lawrence house; if from the Percy Street end, then it was No 12. In Eastwood itself there are partisans of both points of view.

later life Bert Lawrence recalled the delight with which he watched his father make fuses for the explosives used down the pit, neatly cutting wheatstraws and packing them with gunpowder, then sealing them with little pieces of soap. At other times Mr Lawrence would read aloud from the newspapers, stumbling over some of the words and being prompted by his impatient wife. And when Bert and Ada were small he delighted them by bringing home from the fields a baby rabbit, soon christened Adolf. It was Mrs Lawrence who finally expelled Adolf when his droppings became too much of nuisance. She detested pets because they introduced dirt and disorder into her clean, well-run house, though at various times she reluctantly put up with rabbits, rats and a terrier called Rex, left in her charge by the black sheep of her family, her brother Herbert the publican. On the issue of animals, at least, Arthur Lawrence, Bert and the other children were allies in the cause of anarchy and fun.

But all too often Arthur was out for much of the evening, until he staggered back down the road with his friends from the pit, giving a last, slurred rendition of 'Lead, kindly light'. When he came in, his pleasantly fuddled mood soon gave way to brutal, bewildered rage at the tongue-lashing he received from his wife, and there were terrible rows over his drinking and the inadequacies of the housekeeping money. The children could hear their parents' voices raised even above the wind moaning in the old ash tree across the road from the house. Then they would lie awake, dreading to hear thuds and shrieks, and only able to feel secure when their father's footsteps sounded on the stairs, taking him up to bed. Mealtimes could be unpleasant as well. When Mr Lawrence poured his tea into a saucer, blew on it and sucked it up, there would be grimaces of distaste. Provoked, he would make a point of eating and drinking as noisily as possible, deliberately turning himself into the pig his wife and children believed him to be. And from time to time he would simply blow up and rage against the malice of his wife and the ingratitude of his children.

Reading about families like this, it is hard to understand how they could bear staying together — to which part of the answer is that they more or less had to: the family was an economic unit, as well as the unit of respectability. And among the Lawrences, intense strife had a binding effect: 'Home was home, and they loved it with a passion of love, whatever the suffering had been' (*Sons and Lovers*). Furthermore, life is not all quarrels, even in the unhappiest families; and people have an astonishing capacity to go on from day to day, working and bearing things and not even thinking themselves especially unfortunate.

Over the years Mrs Lawrence's life, at any rate, became easier.

79

79 Thomas Philip Barber, the mineowner, was a model for Gerald Crich in *Women in Love*, which includes several incidents from the Barber family's history. Like Crich, Barber was more efficiency-conscious than his father — 'mechanical' in personality and outlook, in Lawrence's view. Like Crich, too, he had accidently killed his own brother. And the fictional incident in which Gerald Crich forces his mare to remain at a level crossing, despite the fact that she is frantic with fear of an approaching locomotive, also derives from an occurrence that involved Philip Barber. Lawrence himself is said to have crossed swords with Barber, who turned him off family property which local people were normally allowed to walk across.

Housekeeping was less of a struggle once the older children began to earn money. In the mid-'nineties Emily left school and stayed home, helping about the house; and as soon as Bert and Ada were old enough to look after themselves, their mother had the time and energy to take up some of her old interests. She read more, becoming absorbed in novels for the first time in many years; she loved Sir Walter Scott's historical tales, which provided a form of high-class escapism, with plenty of noble heroes and pure heroines, and she thrilled to the melodramatics of the great contemporary best-seller, *East Lynne* by Mrs Henry Wood.

Most of the books came from the Mechanics' Institute, a nondescript building just across the road from the Sun Inn; its library held fifteen hundred volumes and was open to borrowers for two hours a week, on Thursday afternoons. There were such institutes in many industrial towns, representing one aspect of working-class self-help. But the first president of the Eastwood Institute, opened in 1863, was Thomas Barber the mineowner, in this as in other respects a patron of the colliers. Among other benefactions the Barbers had built the colliers' houses and set up the gasworks that supplied their homes. The owners' attitudes were in fact much more patriarchal than we might expect to find in the mid-Victorian period, notorious for harsh masters and cut-throat competition. By the 1890s the old relationship was dissolving as the owners became more efficiency-conscious — like Gerald Crich in *Women in Love* — and the colliers more willing to organize and demand rights rather than accept favours. However, the era of great strikes was yet to come, and some of the traditional gestures were still made, including the distribution of oranges and shiny new pennies to the colliers' children at Lamb Close, where they queued up to receive them every Christmas. On at least one occasion the shy Bert had to be helped out by Mabel Thurlby, who went up and collected his presents as well as her own. On the way home he decided that they would give his penny to Mrs Lawrence and buy sweets for themselves with Mabel's money....

Mrs Lawrence's liberation meant that she could now go to the Women's Guild every Monday night. The Guild was an offshoot of the Co-operative Society, and gave the wives of Eastwood an opportunity to write papers on various subjects and read them aloud to the members; later on Bert and Ada remembered the surprise and admiration they felt at seeing their mother pondering her subject and then writing fluently in 'a fine Italian hand'. The colliers rather resented this activity on the part of their womenfolk, dimly sensing that there was danger to male supremacy in any gathering of women to discuss 'ideas'. For a time Lydia Lawrence acted as secretary to the guild, a task that included organizing parties to visit such local beauty spots as Matlock in Derbyshire, for which they hired a brake, a sort of large open cart drawn by a horse.

However, from 1899 intellectual life in Eastwod centred on the Congregational Literary Society founded by Robert Reid. In its heyday it boasted some three or four hundred members, and a popular lecturer could draw an audience of two hundred on a single occasion. Visiting speakers covered an impressive range of subjects from early English drama to the poetry of Tennyson. For their shilling a year, members could also use the chapel to stage debates and socials, and to read papers of their own composition; the opportunity was taken by earnest radicals as well as by Nonconformists (the two were often one and the same), making the society an intellectually lively place that was in time to attract the adolescent Bert and his friends.

But first Bert was to be rescued from drudging at Haywood's — though rescue came in the form of a family tragedy.

Fact into Fiction: 'YOU TOUCHED ME'

'You Touched Me' is one of several Lawrence stories in which the act of touching establishes a bond between two people that transcends their ordinary 'social' feelings about each other. Despite the apparent sophistication of the theme, Lawrence based his descriptions of the setting and characters on Eastwood's Pottery House and Mellor family on Lynn Croft — literally round the corner from his own family home in Walker Street, which had actually been built by the Mellors, and even closer from about 1905 when the Lawrences themselves came to live on Lynn Croft.

80

80 William Mellor. He built the earliest block of Walker Street houses (known locally as 'Mellor's Row'), in one of which the Lawrence family lived.

81 Lynn Croft Pottery and 'Pottery House', home of the Mellor family. The pottery specialized in ink bottles; Mellor paid the men a penny for every board of forty small bottles they produced. The building caught fire in 1893, and the scarred walls can be seen in the photo, just below the bottle chimneys.

Lawrence used both the setting and the family situation in his story 'You Touched Me': 'The Pottery House was a square, ugly, brick house girt in by the wall that enclosed the whole grounds of the pottery itself. To be sure, a privet hedge partly masked the house and its grounds from the pottery-yard and works: but only partly. Through the hedge could be seen the desolate yard, and the many-windowed, factory-like pottery, over the hedge could be seen the chimneys and the out-houses.'

82 Francis Mellor and his wife, surrounded by their family. Top left are Mellor's son-in-law, George Hodgkinson, and his wife Elizabeth; their small daughter Mary is at the front, sitting with Maud Mellor. Maud and her sister Mabel (holding the dog) seem to have provided models for the sisters in Lawrence's 'You Touched Me'.

After the death of his first wife, George Hodgknison married Flossie Cullen (see photographs 58 and 65).

84 Maud Mellor, Mabel's younger sister. 'Emmie was shorter, plumper than her sister, and she had no accomplishments.'

83 Mabel Mellor lived in 'the Pottery House' at Eastwood, like Matilda in Lawrence's 'You Touched Me'. 'Matilda was a tall, thin, graceful, fair girl, with a rather large nose.... She now dressed herself most scrupulously, carefully folded her long, beautiful, blonde hair, touched her pallor with a little rouge, and put her long string of exquisite crystal beads over her soft green dress. Now she looked elegant, like a heroine in a magazine illustration, and almost as unreal.'

VII
A 'New Life'

At the beginning of October 1901 Ernest came home specially to see the Goose Fair at Nottingham. As far as the city was concerned, this was the greatest event of the year, a hectic, noisy, thrilling celebration that filled up the market place and brought all traffic in the city to a standstill for three days. Compared with this, the Eastwood wakes were small and peaceful, and even in London Ernest felt the pull of Goose Fair.

He had not been feeling well for some time. He stayed at Eastwood, and then in Nottingham with his brother George, who went with him after the fair to Nottingham's Victoria Station and saw him off. George was concerned about Ernest's bad cold and inflamed face, and advised his brother to see a doctor and go to bed for a few days. But, conscientious and ambitious as ever, Ernest showed up at the office next day, only to be sent home to his lodgings in South London. Two days later his landlady decided to check on him, and discovered him on the floor of his room, unconscious and dreadfully ill. She telegraphed Ernest's mother, who rushed to London; but he never regained consciousness. The cause of his death was acute inflammation (erysipelas), complicated by pneumonia. He was twenty-three years old.

Mrs Lawrence, though stricken, had the strength of will to make all the necessary arrangements; Arthur Lawrence came up to London for only the second time in his life, but he was too dazed and bewildered to be much help. Ernest's body was taken to Eastwood and he was laid out in his coffin in the parlour of the Walker Street house; and on the fourteenth of October he was buried at the local cemetery.

Lydia Lawrence never completely recovered from the blow; even years later she could never quite enter into the spirit of parties and dances arranged by her other children and their friends. Immediately after Ernest's death she was blankly indifferent to everything but her grief: she even ignored Bert, who seems to have been plunged deeper into misery by this than by his brother's death. But then he too caught pneumonia — an event that, given its timing, looks suspiciously like a desperate attention-getting gesture. Such psychosomatic illnesses occur quite often in over-intense family situations, developing from genuine weak spots — which Lawrence's chest certainly was. The case is made all the more interesting by that fact that, ten years later,

85 The Haggs, the farm run by the Chambers family. For years it was a second home to Lawrence. This interesting photograph shows the farm being visited by his sister Ada, his old friend W.E. Hopkin, and a friend of his later years, the novelist Aldous Huxley.

86 Edmund and Sarah Ann Chambers, tenants of the Haggs, with their children.

another attack of pneumonia made it impossible for him to carry on with an unwanted engagement to marry, and forced him to give up teaching and become a professional writer.

Whatever its origins, Bert's illness put him in mortal danger. His mother was roused from her despair and nursed him heroically until he was on the road to recovery. He was sent to spend a month by the sea at Skegness, where Mrs Lawrence's sister Nellie ran a boarding house, and then came back to Eastwood to finish convalescing.

The following spring and summer he paid many visits to the Haggs, the farm in the Greasley area where the Chambers family lived. Mrs Lawrence had become friendly with Mrs Chambers at the Congregational chapel several years earlier, and in the summer of 1901 she had finally got round to walking the three miles through country lanes that separated the farm from Eastwood. Bert had gone with her, but his

86

87 The British School, where Lawrence worked between 1902 and 1906 as a pupil-teacher, stood in Albert Street, next to the Congregational Church.

work at Haywood's prevented him from seeing much of the Chambers family for a time. Now he virtually fell in love with the whole family, perhaps because the atmosphere of the Haggs seemed to be free from the griefs and tensions that permeated his own home. The Haggs was only a smallholding, and Edmund Chambers supplemented his income by delivering milk around Eastwood. While Bert was still weak, Chambers used to pick him up on his round and drive him to the farm. Bert had a wonderful time there, discussing religion with Chambers, entertaining Mrs Chambers and the seven children with imitations and newly invented games, and helping out around the farm. A little later, when he was stronger, he joined Mr Chambers and his two oldest sons in haymaking; for some time the boys were his closest friends. 'Work goes like fun when Bert's there,' Mr Chambers declared. Mrs Lawrence may have rejoiced to see her son flourish in the country air, but she soon became rather jealous of Bert's impatience to dash off almost every day to the farm which had become his second home and the 'Haggites' who had become as close to him as kin. For years afterwards he visited the Chambers family at least once every week, and towards the end of his life he wrote touchingly to David Chambers of how 'a new life began in me there.... Tell your mother I never forget, no matter where life carries me.... Oh I'd love to be nineteen again, and coming up through the Warren and catching the first glimpse of the buildings. Then I'd sit on the sofa under the window, and we'd crowd round the little table to tea, in that tiny little kitchen I was so at home in.'

The Haggs was only one aspect of the 'new life'. After his illness there was no question of Bert returning to Haywood's or taking up any kind of business career. Instead he was to become a teacher, although this was no easy option in the Lawrences' circumstances. Bert would have to start as a pupil-teacher, spending about half his time teaching and the other half being taught. The system was typically Victorian in ensuring that the training paid for itself in work done by the trainee. The starting salary for Bert was five pounds a year (less that two shillings a week), which meant that Mr and Mrs Lawrence would again have to support him.

Bert was accepted as a pupil-teacher at the British School on the

88 A class photo from the British School at Eastwood, where Lawrence worked as a pupil-teacher. According to the late Sam Alsopp (bottom left), Lawrence taught this class. The adults are the headmaster, Mr Holderness, and his wife.

89 Nottingham Road, Eastwood's main street. Just above Hopkin's shoe shop (right) is Charlie Barker's pork-butcher's shop, where the young pupil-teacher Lawrence earned a little money on Friday nights by making out the customers' weekly bills.

A little further up on the opposite side is George Henry Cullen's London House, a large shop with arched windows.

recommendation of the Reverend Robert Reid. The school itself was something of a cultural centre in Eastwood, and it was soon to offer evening classes in commercial arithmetic, domestic economy and other subjects. It was a peculiar structure in the Neo-Gothic style, built in two halves (one for boys and one for girls) like two medieval chapels side by side. The medieval style was kept up at the expense of lighting: each 'chapel' had three narrow windows overlooking the street, crowned by high oriel windows. Most striking of all in a red-brick area, beneath its slate roof the British School was pale yellow, built entirely of rough-hewn sandstone blocks.

Here Bert Lawrence came every day to teach and study under the headmaster, George Holderness. It was often hard work: Lawrence was not good at maintaining discipline, and at the British School he had to deal with classes of forty unruly boys who were well aware that he was not a 'real' teacher but only a miner's son, just as they were themselves. And working in the same room with several other classes must have destroyed any chance of doing more than teach by rote. But there were compensations: the hours were much shorter than at Haywood's, and Lawrence saved an extra couple of hours a day by working at a place so near his home. To earn a little extra money he

90 Charlie Barker, the butcher.

made out the customers' weekly bills on a Friday night at Charlie Barker's pork-butcher's shop, though he was still sensitive enough to loathe this exposure to the public gaze.

March 1904 brought a change from the hard grind of the British School. The 1902 Act had laid down new regulations, and for part of the week Lawrence was now able to attend a pupil-teacher centre at Ilkeston, just south of Eastwood. This meant a train journey again in the morning, though only a short one: on pleasant days Bert and his friends often walked back to Eastwood through the fields. The friends must have been the nicest feature of the change of system: once all the young pupil-teachers from the Eastwood area went to the same centre, they inevitably got to know one another well and came to think of themselves as a group; according to one of them, George Henry ('Diddler') Neville, they were known as 'the Pagans'. Neville was a close friend from Lawrence's schooldays; Richard Pogmore, Alice Hall and Kitty Holderness, the headmaster's daughter, were fellow-pupils at the British School; and other Pagans included the eldest Chambers boy, Alan, Leonard Watts, and two girls who were later to be Lawrence's neighbours, Gertrude and Frances Cooper.

According to Neville, Flossie Cullen, though not a teacher, was

91

91-2 97 Lynn Croft, the house to which the Lawrences moved when they left Walker Street; the photographs show it as it was in Lawrence's day (91) and as it is now (92). The Lawrences are said to have been persuaded to move to Lynn Croft by Gertrude and Frances Cooper, whose family lived next door, in the house on the right. Their father, Thomas Cooper, was the model for Lawrence's hero in the novel *Aaron's Rod* — at least in externals: like Aaron Sisson he was a skilful flautist and worked as a checkweighman (that is, a man employed by the miners to make sure that the amount of coal they extracted was accurately registered on the masters' scales and recorded).

'almost a Pagan'. Lawrence is said to have been a frequent visitor to the Cullen household, and *The Lost Girl* reveals how closely he observed its curious history. The prop of the entire establishment was Miss Wright (Miss Frost in the novel), who had been Flossie's governess. She continued to live with the family after Flossie had grown up, earning her living as a music teacher; Emily and Ada Lawrence were both among her pupils. Another woman, the tailoress Miss Nichols (Miss

93-5 Two interestingly unconventional photographs of W.E. Hopkin which suggest his adherance to Edward Carpenter's Whitmanesque outdoor philosophy; in one (93) he has a flower in his mouth and is with his daughter Enid.

Hopkin and his wife Sallie were the leaders of Eastwood's small group of 'progressives', who met at the Hopkins' house on Devonshire Drive (94). The young Lawrence was a frequent visitor. He later used Hopkin as a model for characters in *Mr Noon* and the play *Touch and Go,* of which he sent Hopkin a copy inscribed 'Here you are Willie!' The two men remained friends until Lawrence's death. Hopkin was a prominent and respected figure until his own death in 1951. The Hopkin Room in Eastwood Public Library now houses his collection of Lawrence first editions and other materials.

95

96 Hopkin's shoe shop, on Nottingham Road. After his father took over the shop, W.E. Hopkin went to work next door, at the Post Office. He did later manage the shoe shop.

Pinnegar in *The Lost Girl*), effectively ran George Henry Cullen's shop, staying on as housekeeper after it closed. These two ladies seem to have taken over responsibility for London House from the invalid Mrs Lucy Cullen and her erratic husband; Miss Wright was so much part of the family that she was even buried in the Cullen plot in Eastwood Cemetery.

Although eccentrically run, George Henry Cullen's drapery business survived in shrunken form until the deaths of Miss Wright and Lucy Cullen. Then, in his old age, Cullen's craving for a larger sphere of action entirely got the better of him, and he sank his money first into a brickyard, then a windlass pit, and finally a cinema in Langley Mill — all of which Lawrence gleefully recorded in *The Lost Girl*. Some of Cullen's other eccentricities have not been forgotten in Eastwood, notably his habit of carrying a block of wood wrapped in brown paper to local football matches; at the ground he would unwrap his parcel,

put the wood on the earth, and step on to it while neatly folding up the brown paper and storing it away for future use! A living witness, Winnie Brittain, then a child who lived a couple of doors away, recalls visiting Cullen and being fascinated by his way of eating an apple, which he cored with a knife, then consumed with a teaspoon, scooping out the flesh until only the hollow skin was left. She also remembers sitting on his knee and being allowed to plait his long whiskers. Alas, no photograph of this entertaining character seems to exist, although one of the prayers he composed (and in *The Lost Girl* 'James composed beautiful prayers') survives as further evidence of his curious turn of mind.

Ada Lawrence and one of the younger Chambers girls, Jessie, also became members of the 'Pagans' group, though they were a year behind Lawrence and attended the centre on different days from him. Lawrence had encouraged Jessie's ambition to be more than a farm

97 Alice Dax with her husband and children. She was a prominent Eastwood 'progressive' and suffragette, highly unconventional by the standards of the time and place. Lawrence had what may well have been his first significant sexual experience with Alice Dax, who was probably the main model for Clara Dawes in *Sons and Lovers*.

girl, and may well have helped to persuade her parents that she should be allowed to train as a teacher. At this stage in Lawrence's life, Jessie's intensity and intellectual aspirations began to make her even more important to him than other members of the Chambers family. For a time he seems to have been drawn to Jessie's older sister, May — he was certainly jealous of May's fiancé, Will Holbrook, who also became a favourite at the Haggs. And Alan Chambers was Lawrence's close friend from the time of his convalescent haymaking with the family. But Jessie gradually absorbed more and more of Lawrence's attention. Their relationship was intense but problematic; and it remains so for us. Lawrence and Jessie talked over all their ideas and experiences, and read and discussed the same books; and when Lawrence began to write he submitted his work to Jessie for her opinion. But there was no declared romantic attachment and no sex; for some years they were, according to Jessie, 'fierce in virginity', a condition that does not, of course, preclude sexual feelings. A time came when Lawrence, under pressure from his mother, tried to put a

98 Lawrence in 1908, during his time at Nottingham University College.

certain distance between himself and Jessie, citing the example of George Neville, who had 'got a girl in trouble'; but the relationship went on for years in an increasingly tortuous and ambiguous fashion. Whether Jessie failed to attract Lawrence sexually, whether she exaggerated their intimacy, whether he let her down in the end because of his mother's hostility to her — the answers to these and other questions depend on how the reader interprets Lawrence's fictional version of their relations in *Sons and Lovers*, and Jessie's own account of it (after his death) in *D.H. Lawrence: A Personal Record*. The importance of the relationship is not in doubt, however, and in retrospect Lawrence referred to it baldly as a 'betrothal of six years' standing'.

Lawrence's other love, his mother, had never really liked the Walker Street house after Ernest's death, and eventually (probably in 1905) the family moved round the corner to Lynn Croft, next door to the Coopers. This was as close to the suburban middle-class ideal as you could get in Eastwood. It also had many 'extras', such as a little entrance hall, two kitchen ranges (one in the scullery), and a china closet. The whole family was proud of it.

Perhaps that helped to make home a more lively place. Bert and Ada were now more or less grown up, and their friends were often at the

99 Beauvale Priory, one of the landmarks of the 'Lawrence Country' north of Eastwood. In one of his earliest stories, 'Legend' (later retitled 'A Fragment of Stained Glass'), he describes 'the ruins of a Cistercian Abbey. These ruins lie in a still rich meadow at the foot of the last fall of woodland.... Of the Abbey, there remains only the east wall of the chancel standing, a wild thick mass of ivy weighting one shoulder, while pigeons perch in the tracery of the lofty window.'

house. There were sing-songs at the piano and endless games of charades, for which Bert had an unquenchable enthusiasm. Mrs Lawrence, with her characteristic disdainful sniff and dry sarcasms, kept things in order; the young people seem to have shared Bert's admiration for the indomitable 'Little Woman'. She made a point of allowing girls to come and go as they pleased, remarking laconically that there was safety in numbers; she probably hoped that they would counterbalance the influence of Jessie Chambers. On at least one occasion the young Lawrences held a Christmas Eve dance in the garret of the Lynn Croft house. Chinese lanterns were lit, and Bert made sure the floors were waxed, shredding some candles and then sliding about to work them into the floorboards. Then Bert, Ada and their friends danced to the fiddle. There were alarms when the lanterns caught fire, and even greater alarms when Bert took the party down to the parlour and thoroughly frightened them all with a ghost story, aided by a noisy intervention from George Neville.

A few years later, Bert and the other Pagans began to visit William Hopkin's house regularly on Sunday nights. Hopkin was a remarkable man who began life as a colliery clerk and cobbler, and eventually became a local councillor and magistrate. Under the pen-name 'Anglo-Saxon' he wrote a column in the *Eastwood and Kimberley Advertiser*, and in these early years of the century his house was the centre of 'progressive' thought in Eastwood. Hopkin's advocacy of socialism and the suffragette movement influenced many of the Pagans, and it was one emancipationist, Alice Dax, the chemist's wife, who gave Lawrence what was probably his first meaningful experience of sex; the passages concerning 'Clara Dawes' in *Sons and Lovers* suggest that the relationship was neither brief nor unimportant, though little is otherwise known of it.

At Hopkin's house Bert had the opportunity to meet interesting and even eminent socialists; among those who stayed there were such nationally known figures as Keir Hardie, Ramsey Macdonald and the famous Fabians Beatrice and Sidney Webb. All the same, Lawrence's interest in politics was never more than sporadic, whereas religion remained an important preoccupation: by 1907 he was undergoing a crisis of conviction, writing earnestly to the Reverend Reid and finally abandoning belief in a personal God and most of the apparatus of institutional religion.

Some time before this, Lawrence's teaching career took a long step forward. Towards the end of 1904 he sat the King's Scholarship examination and was placed in the top group for the whole of England and Wales. This success opened up the prospect of a university education, and, as Lawrence thought, a dazzlingly different world of intellectual passion. But first he had to serve his last six months as a pupil-teacher and take the London Matriculation examination, which he passed in June 1905. Even then he could not go straight to college because he lacked the twenty pounds in advance fees, payable before he could enroll and collect his scholarship money. So he had to work a further year at the dreary British School while he and his family saved; and it evidently required a tremendous effort on the part of all of them, despite the fact that in November 1904 Emily married a driver, Samuel Taylor King, and moved into a home of her own.

Still, Arthur and Lydia Lawrence had what seems to have been their first seaside holiday in 1906. Bert had had his first sight of the sea earlier, when he recuperated at Skegness, and had been so impressed that he had insisted on taking Ada and the Chambers family there on a day trip. They all ate an exotic fruit, then unknown to Eastwood — the melon. Mr and Mrs Lawrence went to Mablethorpe, which like Skegness is on the Lincolnshire coast. They made up a party of relatives and friends that included Bert and Jessie Chambers; aside from any other consideration, travelling as a group was cheaper. In subsequent years they went to Robin Hood's Bay and Flamborough, on the Yorkshire coast; and then in 1909 Bert — by then a teacher in Croydon — went with his mother and some of the Pagans to Shanklin on the Isle of Wight, where they watched Cowes Regatta and the naval review held in honour of George V and the Russian Tsar. Even for mining folk in the heart of England, life was opening out a little in the early twentieth century.

In September 1906 Lawrence entered Nottingham University College, a massive twenty-five-year-old Gothic edifice, grandiosely built of stone. At first he intended to read for a degree, but he soon switched to the Teacher's Certificate course, which took only two years and did not require him to study Latin. Lawrence had simply become utterly disillusioned with the place: rightly or wrongly, he thought that the lecturers, so far from being intellectually passionate, were conventional mediocrities who merely went through the motions when teaching or discussing their subjects; for his very first essay Lawrence had tried to produce something out of the ordinary run, only to be told to write it again 'properly'. He also loathed teaching practice, since he had to work under a master who trained boys to turn out stereotyped, lifelessly 'correct' essays without the slightest element of creativity. And, being older than most of the students (twenty-one), he resented being treated 'like a kid'. But he stuck it out: he needed his paper qualification too badly to go in for gestures of protest.

However unsatisfying, college meant leisure to read and write. In 1907 Lawrence started work on *Laetitia*, which eventually became his first novel, *The White Peacock*; he wrote poems; and he published his first story. The *Nottinghamshire Guardian* ran a short-story competition, offering three guineas to the winner in each of three categories. Lawrence entered all three. He sent in 'Legend' under his own name, 'The White Stocking' under the name of Louie Burrows, a Derbyshire girl who had joined the Pagans and had also gone on to college, and 'A Prelude' under Jessie's name. It was the sentimental 'Prelude', afterwards disowned by Lawrence, that won the three guineas — his first literary earnings.

In June 1908 Lawrence was awarded a Teacher's Certificate, First Class, and had to face up to the prospect of starting a career.

Picture Essay

The 'Pagans' —
FRIENDS OF LAWRENCE'S YOUTH

During his childhood Lawrence was a frail, timid boy. Other colliers' sons scorned him as a sissy who was usually to be found among the girls, and his strongest emotions were fixed on his mother. But the friendship of the Chambers family at the Haggs Farm helped to make him more outgoing, and from March 1904 he was part of a lively group of fellow-student-teachers, the 'Pagans'.

100 George Henry Neville, whom Lawrence nicknamed 'Diddler'. He was a year younger than Lawrence, whose example he followed by winning a scholarship from Beauvale Board School to Nottingham High School. The boys travelled to and from school together for two years, and became friends. Later, Neville was one of the group of Lawrence's fellow-students who attended the Ilkeston Centre for pupil-teachers. According to Neville, in his *Memoir of D.H. Lawrence: The Betrayal*, these young people were known as 'The Pagans'. Neville was the only one of them to use the term in writing of the period, so it is quite possible that 'Pagans' is a piece of romantic invention, nonetheless, it has become firmly established.

Neville also seems to have exaggerated his closeness to Lawrence, though they did go on holiday together in 1910, staying at a Blackpool boarding house. Lawrence's *alter ego* in *Sons and Lovers*, Paul Morel, also holidays at Blackpool — with Newton, 'a big jolly fellow, with a touch of the bounder about him'. This, like Lawrence's amused description of Neville in a letter as a 'Don Juanish fellow', compelled to marry in haste, suggests that he did

101 Frances and Gertrude Cooper —'Fran' and 'Grit' — were the Lawrences' neighbours, and close friends of D.H. Lawrence. All three were pupil-teachers, travelling regularly to Ilkeston with other young friends. These 'Pagans' included Lawrence's sister Ada, Jessie and Alan Chambers, Louie Burrows, George Henry Neville, Leonard Watts, Richard Pogmore, Kitty Holderness and Alice Hall. All the Cooper sisters were tubercular and died relatively young. Gertrude was a close friend of Ada Lawrence and lived with her at Ripley in the 1920s; she is buried in the Lawrence plot at Eastwood cemetery.

not take him too seriously. However, Lawrence's play *The Married Man*, which features both Neville's domestic situation and Lawrence's own relationship with Frieda Weekley, derived from his stay with Neville in March 1912. Shortly afterwards Lawrence left England, and there seems to have been no further contact between the two men.

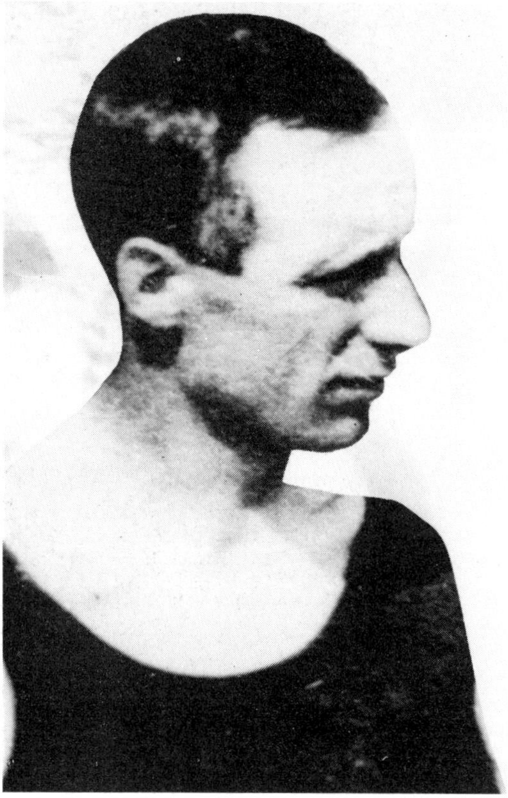

102-3 Leonard Watts (102) and Richard Pogmore (103) were 'Pagans' who made a modest appearance in *Sons and Lovers* as 'Leonard' and 'Dick'. The identification is confirmed by the occasion on which their full initials are given in the book: 'Leonard and Dick immediately proceeded to carve their initials, "L.W." and "R.P.", in the red sandstone.'

104 Class at the British School, about 1904-5. The teacher is Richard Pogmore.

103

105 Alice Hall, one of the 'Pagans' and a frequent visitor to the Lawrence household. D.H. Lawrence put her in his novel *The White Peacock*, somewhat under-disguised as 'Alice Gall'. When the book appeared in 1911 her husband, White Holditch, threatened to sue Lawrence; he was dissuaded by William Hopkin, who convinced him that such an action was inconsistent with his Quaker beliefs. Later, Lawrence put Alice Hall into *Sons and Lovers* and into the play *A Collier's Friday Night*, in both of which she is called Beatrice Wyld — still not much of a 'disguise', since Beatrice was her second name and Wyld her mother's maiden name!

106 Jessie Chambers, the model for Miriam Leivers in *Sons and Lovers*, Emily in *The White Peacock*, and important aspects of Hermione in *Women in Love*. Lawrence's portrait of Miriam wounded Jessie deeply, ending their long, passionate and difficult friendship. Lawrence excused himself by claiming that *Sons and Lovers* embodied artistic rather than literal truth; Jessie's version of the relationship was published anonymously, after Lawrence's death, as *D.H. Lawrence: A Personal Record* (1935) by 'E.T.'

106

Underwood
Schools
1st Class 1909

107 Jessie Chambers with one of her classes.

108 Ada Lawrence as a young woman. Born in 1887, two years after 'Bert' (D.H. Lawrence), she was closest to him of all the family except their mother. She attended the pupil-teacher centre at Ilkeston, though on different days from her brother, and was part of the 'Pagans' group. She taught at the New Eastwood School until her marriage in 1913 to Eddie (William Edwin) Clarke.

VIII
Leaving

Bert Lawrence found himself a teaching job that took him right away from home for the first time. This was semi-deliberate, since he decided he would not accept a salary of less than ninety pounds a year — not a vast sum, but ambitious for a man of Lawrence's age in a poorly paid profession. His friend Louie Burrows found a job straight away — at seventy-five pounds a year. Lawrence expected more after all his years of training, and was perhaps also giving life a chance to tear him away from Eastwood, with its intense family life and network of difficult relationships.

His obstinacy was rewarded: at the last moment, when the autumn term had already begun, he was offered a job at ninety-five pounds a year, and left to work at the Davidson Road School in Croydon, just south of London. His first reaction to teaching and living in digs was

109 Louie Burrows, 'a glorious girl... swarthy and ruddy as a pomegranate', was Lawrence's fiancée from December 1910 to January 1912.

110 Lawrence's mother during her last illness; she died on 9 December 1910. She was nursed by Flossie Cullen, the original of the 'Lost Girl'; D.H. Lawrence presented her with a signed copy of *The White Peacock* as a token of gratitude for her ministrations.

111 Arthur Lawrence, D.H. Lawrence's father, in retirement. In 1911, after his wife's death, he left Lynn Croft and went into lodgings in Bishop Street, just round the corner from Queen's Square, where his daughters Emily and Ada were living. His working life was almost over, as D.H. Lawrence told Louie

112 Emily King, D.H. Lawrence's older sister, with her daughters Joan and Margaret.

Burrows: 'Father is working very little — will soon have done.' Within a few months Lawrence was sending the odd half-crown to Ada for Arthur Lawrence's 'pocket money', and he also insured his father for £9 12s, presumably to pay funeral expenses. However, Arthur Lawrence had a good many years left in him. He eventually went to live with his brother-in-law on Bailey Grove, dying in 1924, only six years before his famous son. This photograph was probably taken at Ripley in Derbyshire, where Arthur Lawrence paid weekly visits to Ada after her marriage in 1913.

one of despair, but by February 1909 he was writing with satisfaction that 'I have tamed my wild beasts.' And London had still more to offer after Jessie Chambers sent some of his poems to *The English Review*, whose editor, Ford Madox Hueffer, took Lawrence up and introduced him to the literary life of the capital.

113 Ada Lawrence and her son Jack. In 1931, after her brother's death, she produced a memoir of him, *Young Lorenzo*, in collaboration with the Nottingham journalist Stuart Gelder. Her son's death from diptheria in a German prisoner of war camp is said to have broken her heart and hastened her own death.

114 The staff of New Eastwood School, where the young Ada Lawrence (seated, right) taught until her marriage in 1913. Her close friend Agatha Kirk (seated, left) appears as Agatha Sharp in D.H. Lawrence's unfinished novel *Mr Noon*.

Emotionally and sexually, however, Lawrence was still uncertain of his direction. No doubt his attachment to his mother helped to make him a late developer (to put the central assertion of *Sons and Lovers* in a rather prosaic fashion). There is plenty of evidence for this view of Lawrence: apart from Jessie's description of their 'fierce virginity', Diddler Neville has recorded Lawrence's shocked disbelief at seeing Neville add armpit and pubic hair to a drawing of a female nude; and as late as 1908 Lawrence wrote to a friend in Liverpool, Blanche Jennings, that 'I have kissed dozens of girls — on the cheek — never on the mouth — I could not.' (This last statement is of course an indication of powerful sexual feelings as well as limited experience.) Not long afterwards he seems to have shed his 'fierce virginity', but without

115 Bromley House, Queen's Square. For some years this was the home of D.H. Lawrence's sister, Emily King. After his mother's death, Lawrence stayed here when he visited Eastwood, in June 1911 and again from February to May 1912 — during which time he met Frieda Weekley, with whom he eloped in May and began a new life.

achieving the kind of stable relationship with a woman that he already felt to be a personal necessity. In 1909 and 1910 he was involved with Jessie Chambers and Alice Dax in Eastwood, as well as with two fellow-teachers at Croydon, Agnes Holt and Helen Corke; but for Lawrence such apparent Don Juanism signified a tormenting failure to make the final connection he craved.

Then in August 1910 Mrs Lawrence fell ill while on a visit to her sister in Leicester. She had to be brought home in a hired car, and Bert rushed to her side. The illness was cancer, and Lydia Lawrence took four months to die. Numb with grief, Lawrence managed to come home from his Croydon job one weekend in every two, nursing his mother devotedly and soothing himself while she slept by sitting painting beside her bed. By October she was 'horribly ill', and Lawrence's writer's eye could not help noticing every detail of her

116 Frieda Weekley, née von Richthofen, who was to become Lawrence's wife. She was married to Ernest Weekley, head of the Department of Modern Languages at Nottingham University College, and is shown here with Montague, one of her three children. Lawrence respected Weekley and sought his advice. Calling at Weekley's house in March 1912, he met Frieda; two months later they eloped to Germany.

face as it collapsed. He was becoming known as an author now, and he begged his publisher to hurry production of his first novel, *The White Peacock*, so that he could put an advance copy in his mother's hands before she died. It was done in time, but Mrs Lawrence was either past caring about anything but her own pain, or unwilling to accept that her son might achieve anything independently of her influence. She looked at the volume for a few moments, and asked to be told what Bert had written in it as a dedication; then it was put away, and she never mentioned it again. His father, told that Lawrence had received fifty pounds for the book, 'looked at me with shrewd eyes, as if I were a swindler. "Fifty pounds! An' tha's niver done a day's hard work in thy life."'

In December 1910, a few days before his mother died, Lawrence proposed to Louie Burrows and was accepted; Louie, he believed, would make a fine wife but (unlike Jessie) would make no demands on his soul — which belonged to his mother. But the dark, statuesque Louie (another 'gypsy', like Ernest's fiancée) proved to be 'awfully good, churchy' and proper, and found Lawrence's urge to give up

117 Nottingham Road, Eastwood's main street. The arched doorway on the left was the butcher's shop; the building on the far right is the cinema, the Eastwood Empire. In 1926 Lawrence wrote in elegiac vein,

'And at the corner of Queen Street, Butcher Bob was huge and fat and taciturn.

Butcher Bob is long dead, and the place is all built up. I am never quite sure where I am, in Nottingham Road.' ('Return to Bestwood')

teaching incomprehensible. For Lawrence, 1911 was an increasingly unhappy year, until illness intervened again to alter the direction of his life. In November he went down with a bad attack of pneumonia, after which a doctor told him he would become consumptive if he went on teaching. So Lawrence was thrown back on writing — and was able to use his poor prospects as an excuse to throw over Louie Burrows.

Although Lawrence's strongest link with Eastwood — his mother — had been broken, he remained in touch with the town, staying with his married sister Emily at her home in Queen's Square and writing regularly to his younger sister, Ada. But in March 1912, during a three-month stay with Emily, he met Frieda Weekley, the German

wife of Ernest Weekley, head of the Department of Modern Languages at Nottingham University College; and their elopement abroad two months later marked the real end of Lawrence's living connection with Eastwood. Even so, he revisited the area occasionally and evidently kept up with some developments there — the silent cinema, the latter-day adventures of George Henry Cullen, the coming of the trams, even the effects of the Great War and the General Strike ('Return to Bestwood'). To the end, his feelings about his family and the town remained ambivalent; only 'the country of my heart' beyond the brick houses always won a good word from him. For better or worse, all three conspired to turn him into 'D.H. Lawrence'.

Fact into Fiction: 'THE WHITE PEACOCK', 'WOMEN IN LOVE' AND 'LADY CHATTERLEY'S LOVER'

The White Peacock (1911) was Lawrence's first novel. It contains many reminiscences of his adolescence, especially the countryside pleasures associated with the Haggs farm and the Chambers family. *Women in Love* (1920) and *Lady Chatterley's Lover* (1928) are more complex and wide-ranging works in which the characters and landscapes tend to be composites. All the same, the history of the Crich family in *Women in Love* closely parallels that of the mine-owning Barbers; and even in *Lady Chatterley* there are some odd and entertaining links with Eastwood and 'the country of my heart'.

118 Felley Mill Farm, the setting for *The White Peacock*; the family at the farm is based on the Chambers, who in fact lived at the Haggs.

119

119-20 Scenes from *The White Peacock* that can be located in the Lawrence country at Newthorpe, just outside Eastwood.

'We [Cyril and George] took the long way home by Greymede, and passed the dark schools. [Bog End School, 119]

"Come on," said he, "let's go in the Ram Inn, [120] and have a look at my cousin Meg." '

120

121 Greasley Parish Church, the 'Willey Green Church' of *Women in Love*, where Laura Crich is married; Ursula sits down on the stone wall of the school, and 'Over the shrubs, before her, were the pale roofs and tower of the church.'

122 Moorgreen crossing. This is evidently where Gerald Crich savagely spurred his Arab mare in *Women in Love*. Moorgreen Reservoir appears in the book as 'Willey Water'. At the beginning of Chapter IX, 'Coal Dust', 'the Brangwen girls descended from the hill between the picturesque cottages of Willey Green till they came to the railway crossing.'

123-4 Two views of Moorgreen Reservoir, where the Barber family held a party every year on Whit Monday. The Reservoir figures as 'Nethermere' in *The White Peacock*, and as 'Willey Water' in *Women in Love*, in which Lawrence based the Crich family on his knowledge of the Barbers: 'Every year Mr Crich gave a more or less public water-party on the lake. There was a little pleasure-launch on Willey Water and several rowing boats, and guests could take tea either in the marquee that was set up in the grounds of the house, or they could picnic in the shade of the great walnut tree at the boat-house by the lake.'

One view (123) shows the side of the Reservoir on which the boat-house stood; this was where the Barbers and their guests spent the day. The colliers employed by Barber, along with their families, were segregated on the other side of the Reservoir (124).

124

123

125

126

125 Robin Hood's Well in High Park; it evidently suggested 'John's Well' in *Lady Chatterley's Lover.* 'She followed the broad riding that swerved round and up through the larches to a spring called John's Well. It was cold on this hillside, and not a flower in the darkness of the larches. But the icy little spring softly pressed upwards from its tiny well-bed of pure, reddish-white pebbles...The place was a little sinister, cold, damp. Yet the well must have been a drinking-place for hundreds of years. Now no more. Its tiny cleared space was lush and cold and dismal.'

127

126 Nottingham Road, Eastwood: a section of the main street between Albert Street and Wellington Street. The high-class grocery in the centre belonged to the West family. On the far right, on the corner of Wellington Street, is the house where the Chatterley family, who are said to have given their name to the Chatterleys in Lawrence's novel.

127 George Chatterley was the Secretary of the Barber, Walker mining company. Local gossip has it that Lawrence asked Chatterley, one of whose daughters was called Connie, whether he would mind his name being used for a character in a novel. Chatterley agreed. His reaction to the scandalous *Lady Chatterley's Lover*, whose heroine is Constance Chatterley, has not been recorded.

128 Devonshire Drive School, Eastwood. In *Lady Chatterley's Lover,* Connie travels through Tevershall (Eastwood), thinking darkly of the ugliness of English life. The climax of her bitter interior monologue is this outburst: 'Just beyond were the new school buildings, expensive pink brick, and gravelled playground inside iron railings, all very imposing, and mixing the suggestion of a chapel and a prison. Standard Five girls were having a singing lesson, just finishing the la-me-doh-la exercises and beginning a "sweet children's song". Anything more unlike song, spontaneous song, would be impossible to imagine: a strange bawling yell that followed the outlines of a tune. It was not like savages: savages have subtle rythms. It was not like animals: animals *mean* something when they yell. It was like nothing on earth, and it was called singing.'

129 The gamekeeper's hut in High Park, the property of the Barber family; it is likely to have been the original of Mellors' hut in *Lady Chatterley's Lover*. 'As she came out of the wood on the north side, the keeper's cottage, a rather dark, brown stone cottage, with gables and a handsome chimney, looked uninhabited, it was so silent and alone.'

Acknowledgements

The authors are grateful to the following who have kindly loaned or donated photographs for use in this book:
Mr Alan Allsopp; Mrs I. Beeken; late Mrs Bricknell; Mr R. Buxton; Mrs M. Chambers; Mr S. Clarke; Mrs A. Crooks; D.H. Lawrence Society; Eastwood Historical Society; Eastwood Town Council; Mrs E. Goodband; Mrs M. Hill; Heanor Historical Society; Mr K. Hodgkinson; Mrs O. Hopkin; Mr R. Johnson; Mr A. Kirk; Mrs J. Lodge; Mrs M. Martin; National Coal Board; Mrs Margaret Needham and Miss Joan King; Nottingham City Library; Nottingham Evening Post; Mr R. Parker; Mr B.R. Russell; Mr G. Shaw; Mr F. Smith; Mr M. Smith; Mrs W. Stoakes; Mrs H.G. Street; Mrs Templeman; Mrs D. Welch; Mr R. Wilson; Mrs G. Winsor; Mr S.C. Wyld; and also to Mr Michael Bennett and the staff of the Eastwood Library for their valuable assistance.

It has proved impossible to trace the source of some of the photographs, and grateful thanks are therefore also given to anyone inadvertantly omitted from the above list.

Bibliography

Books and shorter pieces by and about D.H. Lawrence are now numerous enough to constitute a good-sized specialist library. The items listed here are confined to imaginative or factual accounts of Lawrence's early experience and background.

By Lawrence himself

The White Peacock. Novel. Heinemann, 1911.
Sons and Lovers. Novel. Duckworth, 1913.
The Lost Girl. Novel. Secker, 1920
Women in Love. Novel. Privately printed, 1920; Secker, 1921.
Aaron's Rod. Novel. Selzer (New York), 1922.
Lady Chatterley's Lover. Novel. Privately printed, Florence, 1928; first complete edition published in the USA by Grove Press, 1959; in Britain by Penguin Books, 1960.
Mr Noon. Unfinished novel. First complete British edition published by Cambridge University Press, 1984.
The Complete Short Stories (Heinemann, 3 vols, 1955; also available in five Penguin volumes) include autobiographical and local-descriptive pieces such as 'Rex', 'Adolf', 'A Fragment of Stained Glass', 'The Horse Dealer's Daughter', 'You Touched Me', 'The Christening', 'Her Turn', 'Strike Pay', 'The Miner at Home', and 'Tickets, Please'.
The Complete Plays of D.H. Lawrence. Heinemann, 1965.
The Letters of D.H. Lawrence, vol 1. Cambridge University Press, 1979.
A Selection from Phoenix (edited by A.A.H. Inglis). Penguin Books, 1971. This is the most convenient place to find such essays and articles by Lawrence as 'Autobiographical Sketch', 'Hymns in a Man's Life', 'Nottingham and the Mining Countryside', 'On Coming Home' and 'Return to Bestwood'.

By contemporaries who knew the young Lawrence

Ada Lawrence and G. Stuart Gelder. *Young Lorenzo: The Early Life of D.H. Lawrence.* Orioli, Florence, 1931; published in Britain as *The Early Life of D.H. Lawrence,* Secker, 1932.
Jessie Chambers (under the pseudonym 'E.T.'). *D.H. Lawrence: A Personal Record.* Cape, 1935.
Edward Nehls *D.H. Lawrence: Composite Biography.* University of Wisconsin Press, Madison, 1957.
G.H. Neville. *A Memoir of D.H. Lawrence: The Betrayal* (edited by Carl Baron). Cambridge University Press, 1981.

J.C.P. Taylor. 'Boys of the Beauvale Breed'. Articles in the *Eastwood and Kimberley Advertiser,* 30 December 1960 to 17 August 1962.

Secondary sources and local material

Bridget Pugh. *The Country of My Heart: A Local Guide to D.H. Lawrence.* Nottinghamshire Local History Council, 1972.

Michael Bennett. *A Visitor's Guide to Eastwood and the Countryside of D.H. Lawrence.* Nottinghamshire County Library, 1973.

Roy Christian. *Nottinghamshire.* Batsford, 1974.

Harry T. Moore. *The Priest of Love: A Life of D.H. Lawrence.* Heinemann, 1974.

Philip Callow. *Son and Lover: The Young Lawrence.* Bodley Head, 1975.

Nathaniel Harris. *The Lawrences.* Dent, 1976.

Noel M. Kader. *W.E. Hopkin.* Brittain & Sons, Ripley, 1977.

Norman Page (editor). *D.H. Lawrence: Interviews and Recollections.* 2 vols, Macmillan, 1981.

Keith Sagar. *The Life of D.H. Lawrence.* Eyre Methuen, 1980.

Keith Sagar (editor). *A D.H. Lawrence Handbook.* Manchester University Press, 1984.

The D.H. Lawrence Society, c/o 8A Victoria Street, Eastwood, publishes an annual *Journal* containing new information and other items.

Index

Fictional people and places are in quotation marks, as are titles of short stories. Titles of novels and plays are in italics